SHAREHOLDER
DEMOCRACY

D1547731

SHAREHOLDER DEMOCRACY

A Primer on Shareholder Activism and Participation

Lisa M. Fairfax

CAROLINA ACADEMIC PRESS

Durham, North Carolina

Library of Congress Cataloging-in-Publication Data

Fairfax, Lisa M.
  Shareholder democracy : a primer on shareholder activism and
participation / Lisa M. Fairfax.
    p. cm.
  ISBN 978-1-59460-919-0 (alk. paper)
  1. Stockholders--Legal status, laws, etc.--United States. 2. Cor-
porations--Investor relations--United States. 3. Stockholders' vot-
ing--Law and legislation--United States. 4. Corporate governance-
-Law and legislation--United States. I. Title.
  KF1448.F35 2011
  346.73'0666--dc22
                        2011016326

CAROLINA ACADEMIC PRESS
700 Kent Street
Durham, North Carolina 27701
Telephone (919) 489-7486
Fax (919) 493-5668
www.cap-press.com

Printed in the United States of America
2016 Printing

*This book is dedicated in loving memory to
Horace and Gussie Odom, 'till we meet again...*

CONTENTS

Acknowledgments

Thank you so much to Zoë Oakes, Kelly Miller, Suzanne Morgen, Keith Sipe and the rest of the team at Carolina Academic Press for their hard work on this book, for believing in this project, and for their patience. It was very much appreciated.

Special thanks to Carol Hansell and Anita Anand for their help in connecting me with experts in Canadian law. I also would like to thank Eleanor Farrell and Philipe Tardiff for taking the time to provide me with advice and assistance with respect to shareholder rights and activism in Canada, particularly for their insights with respect to proxy access issues in Canada. Thanks to David Bennett for excellent research assistance.

My heartfelt thanks for the love of my family who supported me throughout this project and support me in all things: to my husband Roger for your support in this and everything I do — I will love you always; to my daughters Fatima, Regina, and Nadia, you are my source of inspiration and I am proud of all that you do — "don't be a hard rock when you truly are a gem..."; to my mom Elizabeth, I love you so much for always believing in me and showing me that I can shine; to my mother-in-law Charlene, thank you for making me a part of your family; to my brothers Omar and Ischmael, you are the best and never ever far from my heart; thank you to my other brothers Chris, Justin, and Darrin; special thanks to Cerina, Jennifer, and Virginia, you are the sisters I always wanted, thank you so much for your support; to my Aunt Barbara, Charlene, and Tanya, thank you for always being there; to my dad, the writing is for you — I love you; to LaMonica Denise, you have never let me down and for that I am always grateful; and to all of my other relatives too numerous to name, but always in my heart, thank you for your guidance, support, and encouragement.

SHAREHOLDER
DEMOCRACY

CHAPTER 1

INTRODUCTION

I. The Subject Matter in General

Increased shareholder power is one of the most significant corporate governance phenomenons of our decade not only because it threatens to alter the corporate balance of power between managers and shareholders, but also because it challenges the traditional board-centric model of corporate governance. In short, increased shareholder power has the potential to impact the manner in which every modern public company had conducted business. And thus, it is a phenomena not to be ignored.

It has long been true that shareholders have desired to gain more power over corporate affairs. Recently this desire has transformed into an aggressive campaign to secure such power. In order to increase their power over director elections, shareholders have pressed for a host of changes including (a) a rule requiring that director candidates must receive a majority of the vote to be elected, (b) the annual election of directors, and (c) "proxy access"—shareholder access to the corporate "ballot" to nominate director candidates of their choice. Shareholders also have expended considerable funds waging election contests to challenge incumbent directors and their policies. In addition, shareholders have sought to enhance their role over executive compensation decisions by pushing for "say on pay"—an advisory vote on executive compensation packages.

Corporate governance scandals and the late-2000's global financial crisis not only spur shareholder efforts to enhance their power, but also increase the appeal of shareholder empowerment. Shareholder activists and legislators argue that such scandals and crisis reflect a lack of sufficient director and officer accountability. In other words, such events suggest that corporate directors and officers felt free to engage in risky transactions or otherwise ignore their obligation to act in the best interest of the corporation and its shareholders *because* no one held them appropriately accountable for their actions. Increased shareholder power, especially increased shareholder voting power, is aimed at addressing this accountability failure by enhancing shareholders' ability to hold directors and officers responsible for their misdeeds.

Because it appears to have the potential to positively address corporate misconduct, shareholders' efforts to increase their voting power have found legislative support. Congress has passed various measures aimed at enabling shareholders to play a larger role in the corporation, from mandating say on pay at all public companies, to specifically authorizing the Securities and Exchange Commission (the "SEC") to implement proxy access rules. The SEC and national securities exchanges also have passed measures aimed at facilitating shareholders' ability to exercise their voting power.

Shareholder activism has yielded success, at least as measured by its impact on generating changes within corporations. Shareholder campaigns have garnered a record level of support from other shareholders, and that support has prompted corporations to implement many shareholder-supported reforms, including those that impact the board and its operations. As a result, shareholder activism has led to significant changes in the corporate governance landscape.

Shareholders' increased activism challenges the traditional assumptions about shareholders and their interactions with the corporation. The traditional assumption is that shareholders are rationally apathetic. The shareholder class at any public company is comprised of a large group of dispersed investors, whose individual vote only may have a small impact on the company. As a result, there appears to be little benefit for shareholders to incur the costs associated with gaining familiarity with a company and its policies. Consequently, it is rational for shareholders to be passive investors who rely on management to govern the corporation. From this perspective, shareholders not only rarely vote, but also rely heavily on managerial recommendations when they choose to vote.

The recent surge in shareholder activism belies this perspective. Shareholders—or at least a significant portion of shareholders—have been neither passive nor content to rely exclusively on corporate officers and directors to run corporate America or otherwise guide shareholders' voting decisions.

This book examines the role of shareholders in corporations and how that role has evolved, giving readers a better understanding of shareholder activism and the debate surrounding its propriety. The book begins with a discussion of the manner in which shareholders exercise their voting power, and the hurdles they confront in such an exercise. After examining the alternative ways in which shareholders can influence corporate affairs, the book then sets forth the cases for and against increasing shareholder power. Importantly, this book focuses on shareholder copyrights. The book discusses the various shareholders that have engaged in activism, as well as the various ways that shareholders have sought to augment their vote. This book uses the terms "managers" or "management" to refer to directors and officers collectively.

It is not clear if shareholders will continue their activism. Even if they do not, however, their efforts have already permanently altered the corporate governance landscape and definitively shifted the balance of power within corporations. This book provides an accessible and comprehensive analysis of those alterations and changes.

CHAPTER 2

SHAREHOLDER VOTING RIGHTS AND LIMITATIONS

This chapter explores the manner in which shareholders exercise their voting rights, and the obstacles that exist to effective exercise of those rights. Before delving into how shareholders exercise their voting rights, this section discusses the sources of those rights.

I. Regulations Impacting Shareholder Rights

A. State Law

State law is the primary source of shareholders' voting rights. That law governs the matters on which shareholders can vote, as well as the process by which shareholders can vote, including the percentage of votes necessary for shareholder approval of particular actions. State law also dictates procedures for annual and special shareholders' meeting, including when and where such meetings must be held, who may call such meetings, the manner in which such meetings must be conducted, and the extent to which shareholder actions can be taken without such meetings. State law also determines the process by which a shareholder can appoint a proxy authorized to vote on the shareholder's behalf.

Importantly, state law governs shareholders' voting rights with respect to electing directors. That law proscribes the portion of votes necessary to elect directors as well as the process by which shareholders may remove directors or fill vacancies on the board. State law also dictates the type of terms directors may have—that is, whether directors must be elected annually or if they may have staggered terms. Through its regulation of director qualifications, state law governs the type of directors shareholders can elect onto the board.

Delaware state law serves as a critical source of guidance in the corporate law arena. Delaware is the incorporation home of more than 50% of *Fortune* 500 companies and is the acknowledged state law leader with respect to the creation and development of corporate law. In 1940 the American Bar Association's Committee on Corporate Laws of the Business Law Section developed a Model Business Corporation Act (the "Model Act"). Thirty states have adopted the Model Act in whole or in substantial part, and thus it also is a significant source of general corporation law.

B. Federal Law

Until the early 1930s, corporate law was a matter left almost exclusively to states. However, the 1929 stock market crash generated concerns about securities fraud and corporate malfeasance, prompting Congress to create federal laws regulating corporations. Congress passed the Securities Act of 1933 (the "Securities Act"), followed by the Securities Exchange Act of 1934 (the "Exchange Act"). A primary thrust of the acts is disclosure, and hence such acts require disclosure of critical information to shareholders so that they can make informed investment decisions. The Exchange Act created the SEC with broad authority to regulate the securities industry.

Because they regulate securities transactions, these federal securities laws impact shareholders and their voting rights. Importantly, most public company shareholders vote by proxy, and Rule 14a of the Exchange Act regulates the proxy solicitation process.[1] That regulation includes provisions implicating shareholders' ability to present proposals at the annual meeting as well as shareholders' ability to nominate directors. Such regulation also addresses the process by which public company shareholders can wage an election contest, known as a proxy contest. Hence, federal law plays a vital role in regulating shareholder voting procedures in the public domain.

In 1940, Congress passed rules regulating investment companies — entities such as mutual funds, that engage in investing or reinvesting securities — and advisors to these companies. The Investment Company Act of 1940 (the "Investment Company Act") requires disclosures on investment companies' financial condition and investment strategies. It also places limits on the kinds of activities in which investment companies can engage. The Investment Advisers Act of 1940 (the "Investment Advisers Act") governs the actions of those who give advice about investment decisions. Because many investment companies are shareholders, both the Investment Company Act and the Investment Advisers Act have a direct impact on shareholder rights.

Another important source of federal law in this area stems from the national securities exchange, such as the New York Stock Exchange ("NYSE") and NASDAQ. Such exchanges have listing standards that impact shareholders and their voting rights. For example, such exchanges mandate that the board of directors and certain board committees be comprised solely of independent members. This mandate impacts the types of directors shareholders can elect. National securities exchanges also regulate the actions of brokers and other intermediaries. A significant percentage of shareholders purchase their shares through brokers. Thus, exchange rules governing brokers implicate shareholders' voting rights. The SEC has authority over the various securities exchanges, and thus can direct such exchanges to implement changes that impact shareholders and their voting rights.

Although these federal laws have played a role in corporate affairs since the 1930s, that role was relatively limited. However, recent federal regulations reflect significant intrusion into state law's traditional dominance over corporate governance and shareholder rights. The federal government has expanded its role in corporate affairs largely in response to seemingly widespread failures in the financial and corporate governance system. Thus, in 2002, in response to accounting and governance scandals such as Enron and WorldCom, Congress passed the Sarbanes-Oxley Act ("Sarbanes-Oxley" or "SOX"), described as incorporating "the most far-reaching reforms of American business practices since the time of Franklin

Delano Roosevelt." Sarbanes-Oxley mandated a host of corporate governance reforms that directly and indirectly implicate shareholders' voting rights. For example, Sarbanes-Oxley imposed independence and literacy requirements related to audit committee members, which impacts the type of directors on which shareholders can vote. Sarbanes-Oxley also directed the national securities exchanges to create governance requirements related to director independence that directly impact shareholders.

The federal government's response to the financial crisis and recession that emerged in 2008 also expanded the government's role in corporate governance. In 2008, Congress passed the Emergency Economic Stabilization Act, updated and extended in 2009 by the American Recovery and Reinvestment Act, which created the Troubled Asset Relief Program ("TARP") to help promote and stabilize the financial markets. TARP enables the federal government to purchase or insure up to $700 billion of assets from financially troubled companies. TARP also imposes corporate governance and other requirements on companies that receive TARP funding. In particular, every company receiving TARP funds must give its shareholders an annual say on pay. Although TARP is not permanent, it is possible that governance charges will remain even after corporations are no longer subject to TARP's requirements.

In 2010, Congress passed the Dodd-Frank Wall Street Reform and Consumer Protection Act ("Dodd-Frank"), referred to as "one of the most sweeping set of financial reforms since the Great Depression." Dodd-Frank embodies far-reaching changes to the financial and securities industry. It also contains a host of provisions aimed at enhancing corporate governance practices. For example, Dodd-Frank requires all public corporations to provide shareholders with a say on pay, and specifically authorizes the SEC to generate rules granting shareholders' access to the corporation's proxy statement to nominate directors of their choice.

The federal law intrusion into corporate law issues has prompted concerns about the propriety of the so-called "federalization" of corporate law. Proponents insist that corporate governance scandals reveal the necessity of federal rules to provide a check on managerial misconduct. Proponents also insist that federal laws are necessary to counteract the "race to the bottom" among state corporate laws. In their view, states have an incentive to adopt corporate statutes favoring directors and officers at the expense of shareholders in an effort to retain the tax revenue generated by charters, creating a race to the bottom among states. As a result, federal law is necessary to ensure proper protection of shareholder rights and to prevent the pro-management bias that may occur at the state level. Critics of federal regulation of corporate governance question the validity of the race to the bottom theory, arguing not only that states have incentives to protect shareholders, but also that state statutes reflect such protection. Moreover, opponents of enhanced federal influence insist that too often federal law generates one-size-fits-all solutions to complex governance problems, which undermines innovation. These critics also insist that states, particularly Delaware, are better experienced and positioned to craft governance rules that respond to the needs of shareholders and corporate managers.

Notwithstanding this insistence, corporate scandals inevitably provide the necessary impetus for enhanced federal intrusion in this area. These scandals therefore have made increased federalization a permanent feature of the corporate governance lexicon.

C. Private Ordering

Because many state law rules are default, corporations and shareholders can contract around them or engage in what is known as "private ordering." Corporate managers and shareholders engage in private ordering through adoption or amendment of provisions in the company's governing documents, including the articles of incorporation or corporate charter, the bylaws, and any shareholder agreement. Under federal law, private ordering occurs primarily through the shareholder proposal process, which enables shareholders to recommend changes to corporate practices or documents.

Many corporate governance experts favor private ordering, particularly as opposed to mandated federal rules. Private ordering gives shareholders the ability to choose the type of governance structure they desire, and thus ensures that they are not left with a one-size-fits-all model of the corporation.

Nevertheless, private ordering may not be the optimal solution for every governance problem. Indeed, in adopting proxy access rules, the SEC pointed out that mandated limitations on private ordering are an acceptable part of corporate governance at the state and federal level. The SEC also stressed that there are some shareholder protections that should not be contracted away by other shareholders. Then too, private ordering may prove costly for shareholders, particularly if there are obstacles associated with shareholders' ability to bargain with corporations to change the default rules. This cost may prevent shareholders from making changes that they desire. In these ways, it is not clear that all shareholders can effectively engage in private ordering.

Ultimately, corporate governance represents a mix of state law, federal law, and private ordering. However, the nature of that mix is constantly in flux.

II. Shareholders' Voting Power in the Corporation

Although the shareholder voting right has been described as fundamental, it is relatively limited. This is because state statutes provide that the corporation is managed by or under the direction of the board of directors. State corporate law provides that the board exercises most of the power and control within the corporation. By comparison, shareholders have limited voting rights, and hence a more limited ability to influence corporate affairs. As a general matter, shareholder voting rights within the corporation cover four spheres: (1) director elections, (2) governing documents, (3) fundamental changes, and (4) conflict of interest transactions. This section discusses these spheres as well as the limitations and impediments to shareholders' exercise of their voting rights.

A. Director Elections

State law governs shareholders' rights with respect to elections. Under state law, shareholders have the right to nominate, elect, and remove directors. Directors are generally elected at the annual meeting or, in the event of a mid-term vacancy, at a special meeting called to fill the vacancy. Some companies have a staggered or classified board pursuant to which a certain percentage of the board is elected each year. As a result, directors serving on a classified board serve multi-year terms, and each year shareholders elect those directors whose terms have expired. With respect to removal, directors can be replaced at the annual meeting or they can be removed at a special meeting called for such a purpose. Directors can be removed with or without cause.

Courts view shareholders' rights with respect to elections as a critical form of board accountability. First, shareholders' ability to impact director elections holds directors accountable, ensuring that directors govern the corporation in a manner that pays heed to shareholder concerns. Second, shareholders' ability to influence director elections indirectly influences the corporation's business decisions. Importantly, shareholders do not have the right to interfere with the board's management function or specific corporate decisions. Thus, shareholders cannot dictate the appointment or removal of officers. Shareholders also cannot direct the board to engage in particular business transactions or lines of business. However, shareholders' ability to elect and remove directors may indirectly influence directors' decisions. In these ways, shareholders' rights over director elections help ensure that boards consider shareholder concerns when carrying out their responsibilities.

However, there are several practical and legal limits on shareholders' director election right. First, restrictions on shareholders' ability to call special meetings may undermine their director election right. As a general rule, shareholders who are discontent with directors must wait until the annual meeting to oust directors. This is because directors can only be removed at the annual meeting or at a special meeting called for such a purpose. State laws and corporate policies place restrictions on shareholders' ability to call special meetings.

Some states leave the issue regarding special meetings to the discretion of the board. For example, Delaware law provides that special meetings may be called by the board or by those who are authorized to hold such meetings in the articles of incorporation or bylaws. Pursuant to such provision, some Delaware corporations only enable the board to call a special meeting. Instead of leaving the issue in the hands of the board, some states restrict the ability to call a special meeting to shareholders who individually or collectively hold a specific percentage of shares. For example, the Model Act provides that holders of at least 10% of a company's shares can call a special meeting, unless a company's articles provide for a lower percentage or a higher percentage not to exceed 25%. Many companies that enable shareholders to call special meetings require that shareholders hold at least 25% of the outstanding shares. Because removing directors mid-stream is linked with the right to call special meetings, restrictions on this right undermine shareholders' ability to fully impact director elections. Shareholders recently have pushed companies to reduce restrictions on special meetings so that shareholders only need to hold 10% of the company's shares in order to call special meetings.

Second, classified boards may hamper shareholders' election right. A classified board prevents shareholders from replacing an entire board during one election cycle. It also undermines shareholders' ability to replace a majority of the board for at least two years.

Finally, shareholders' inability to nominate directors on the corporate proxy statement may undermine the effectiveness of their state law right to nominate and elect directors. Most shareholders in public companies vote by proxy, and thus such shareholders vote for directors who are presented to them on the corporate proxy statement. Proxy rules historically prevented shareholders from nominating candidates of their choice on the corporate proxy statement. Shareholders who sought to nominate candidates of their choice had to create and distribute their own separate proxy statement. Costs and other hurdles made the distribution of such a separate proxy statement difficult for most shareholders. Importantly, because shareholders generally only vote for those candidates who are nominated on the corporate proxy statement, the prohibition on shareholders' proxy nominations also meant that shareholders generally only elected directors who had been nominated by directors and management. From this perspective, prohibiting shareholders from using the corporate proxy statement has been viewed as a significant road-block on shareholders' ability to exercise their nomination and election right. As Chapter 9 reveals, in 2010 the SEC adopted rules facilitating shareholders' access to the proxy statement for purposes of nominating directors of their choice. Implementation of these rules has been placed on hold pending resolution of the lawsuit challenging their validity. However, such rules are aimed at removing hurdles associated with shareholders' state law right to nominate and elect directors.

B. Governance Documents

Shareholders have the ability to vote on amendments to the corporation's two primary governing documents: the charter and the bylaws. Shareholders must approve any amendments to the charter. However, this does not include the right to propose new amendments to the articles. Instead, the board must propose any amendments to the charter, and then shareholders must approve such amendments.

Shareholders have broader rights with respect to bylaws. Most corporations enable shareholders to propose, amend, or repeal bylaws. Corporation statutes generally provide that bylaws may contain any provision relating to the business of the corporation, the conduct of its affairs, or the rights and powers of shareholders or corporate actors. This provision appears to grant shareholders wide discretion to amend the corporation's bylaws in a manner that requires the board to adopt particular actions or engage in specific transactions.

However, this discretion is not as broad as it would appear. First, corporate statutes also grant directors the power to propose and alter bylaws, and thus shareholders' rights in this area co-exist with the board's power. Recently, the Model Act and several corporate statutes have been amended to provide that if shareholders adopt a bylaw provision increasing the amount of votes required to elect a director, such a provision cannot be altered by the board. This amendment is specifically designed to ensure that the board cannot change a shareholder-implemented bylaw requiring that directors can only be elected by a majority of the vote. However, this amendment does not apply to other matters, leaving directors with the ability to alter other shareholder-implemented bylaw changes.

Second, bylaws must be consistent with state law. Because state law grants directors—and not shareholders—the power to manage the affairs of the corporation, bylaw amendments that seek to usurp this power conflict with state law and thus are not valid.

Finally, shareholders can only propose changes to the bylaws at the annual meeting or a special meeting called for such a purpose. Hence, restrictions related to special meetings also restrict shareholders' ability to exercise their bylaw powers.

C. Fundamental Transactions

Shareholders also vote on certain fundamental transactions. Such transactions include mergers, consolidations, dissolution, and a sale of all or substantially all of the corporate assets. Although this vote enables shareholders to have a direct voice in particular business decisions, it is limited in at least three important ways. First, it does not cover ordinary business decisions, which constitute the bulk of corporate actions. Second, such a vote does not include the power to propose fundamental changes. Instead, it reflects shareholders' ability to approve or disapprove of transactions crafted by the directors and officers. Third, shareholder approval with respect to these transactions often requires a "supermajority" of the vote. While corporate statutes generally require that shareholders approve fundamental transactions by a majority of the vote, those statutes also give corporations the discretion to increase (but not decrease) the percentage of votes necessary for approval. Many corporations require such transactions to be approved by a supermajority of the vote—as much as 60% or 75% of the shareholder vote—making it more difficult for shareholders to authorize them. As with special meetings, shareholders have been pressuring corporations to eliminate supermajority requirements and reduce the percentage of votes necessary for approval of fundamental transactions.

D. Conflict of Interest Transactions

Shareholders also play a role in conflict of interest transactions, though that role can be limited. When directors or officers engage in transactions that represent conflicts of interest, one way to validate the transaction is to get approval from the shareholders. Because satisfactory shareholder approval can insulate an otherwise conflicted transaction from legal challenges, this right can be especially important when corporations choose to utilize it. However, corporations are not required to secure this vote. Moreover, like the vote regarding fundamental transactions, this vote does not give shareholders the ability to shape transactions, but rather only enables shareholders to approve or disapprove of them. Hence, shareholder voting in this area may be important, but is also relatively restricted.

E. Other Matters

Corporations also may seek shareholder approval of other matters so long as they are proper subjects for shareholder action. This includes matters for which shareholder approval is required under federal law, such as the annual ratification of independent public accountants, approval of shareholder proposals, and most recently, approval of executive compensation packages.

III. Process by Which Shareholders Vote

A. Shareholder Meetings

1. *Physical Meetings*

Shareholders vote either during an annual meeting or a special meeting. State law governs the procedures for holding meetings and determining which shareholders are allowed to participate in the meeting. As a general matter, corporations set a "record" date, which is the official date on which shareholders must own their shares in order to be eligible to vote at a meeting. With respect to special meetings, corporate statutes allow boards to call special meetings; however, they differ regarding shareholder rights in this area. Some statutes enable the board to determine whether and under what circumstances shareholders can call a special meeting. Other statutes provide that only shareholders holding a specified percentage of shares can call a special meeting. That percentage generally ranges from 10% to 25%. The purpose of a special meeting must be identified in the meeting notice.

Corporations increasingly have used electronic media when conducting their meetings. Thus, a significant number of corporations web-cast their meetings.[2] Moreover, many corporations not only allow shareholders to electronically participate in the meeting, but also enable them to cast their votes electronically.

2. *Virtual Meetings*

Several states allow corporations to conduct virtual or remote-only meetings — that is, meetings that do not occur in a physical setting, but rather solely through means of remote communication.[3] In 2000, Delaware became the first state to pass a statute providing for such meetings so long as the corporation (a) implements procedures to verify who is present and permitted to vote, (b) provides a reasonable opportunity for all shareholders to participate, and (c) ensures that there is a proper record of all shareholder action.[4] As of the end of 2010, twenty-three states have implemented similar provisions.[5] As a general matter, boards have the discretion to decide if they will host an electronic meeting; shareholders cannot demand that corporations conduct meetings remotely.

Remote-only meetings have both benefits and drawbacks. Such meetings have the potential to increase participation by shareholders who may not otherwise be able to travel to the annual meeting. They also may enable corporations to reduce the cost of hosting a meeting at a physical location. However, shareholders express concern that by removing the ability of shareholders to have face-to-face interactions with corporate managers, remote-only meetings enable corporations to ignore shareholder concerns. Hence, many shareholder activists have opposed such meetings. The controversy surrounding remote-only meetings has resulted in very few corporations choosing to conduct remote-only meetings. As of June 1, 2010, only 12 public corporations had hosted remote-only meetings.[6]

B. Voting Matters

1. Required Votes

A shareholder vote is only proper if there is a quorum — the minimum number of shares necessary to conduct business at the meeting. A quorum is usually a majority of the outstanding shares. Once there is a quorum, the precise amount of the required vote differs depending on the issue to be voted upon.

Under most corporate statutes, the default rule is that shareholders vote for directors under a plurality system. This system means that a director is elected so long as she receives a plurality of the votes cast, without regard to votes cast against her or withheld. As Chapter 6 reveals, many corporations have now adopted some form of majority voting for directors pursuant to which directors must be elected by a majority of the shareholder vote.

With respect to fundamental transactions, the default rule is majority vote. However, most corporations have altered that rule to require a higher percentage of shareholder vote, ranging from 60% to 75%. Other matters such as shareholder proposals and approval of public accountants generally only require a majority of the shareholder vote.

2. Actions without a Meeting

In lieu of a meeting — either physical or electronic — a corporation can obtain shareholder approval of an action through written consent. Historically, actions without a meeting required shareholders' unanimous written consent. However, most statutes now have abandoned this rule of unanimity. Instead, statutes enable corporations to adopt a provision in the charter providing for actions to be taken without a meeting so long as the action receives the written consent of the shares that would have been required to authorize the action at the meeting.

3. Electronic Voting

Most corporations currently allow their shareholders to vote electronically. Such electronic voting can take various forms. Some corporations establish toll free numbers. Others allow shareholders to submit their proxies electronically. Still others establish a website that enables shareholders to vote online.

C. Proxy Voting and E-Proxy

Shareholders in public companies vote by proxy. This means that they confer on someone else the ability to vote on their behalf at the annual meeting. While state law governs shareholders' voting rights, as Chapter 9 reveals, federal law governs the proxy solicitation process. Hence, voting in public companies involves the interaction of state and federal law.

The federal proxy rules require that those soliciting shareholders' proxies create and distribute a proxy statement containing, among other things, information about the matters to be voted upon. Proxy statements must be filed with the SEC and distributed to solicited shareholders. As Chapter 7 reveals, the process of creating and distributing a proxy statement can be expensive, particularly when there are competing solicitations, and hence a proxy contest.

In 2007 the SEC implemented rules aimed at facilitating the electronic distribution of proxy materials, known as "e-proxy rules."[7] The SEC phased in the rules so that large companies became subject to the rules a year before other companies. Beginning on January 1, 2009, every public company had to disseminate proxy materials in compliance with the e-proxy rules.

The e-proxy rules enable corporations to follow several different models for electronic delivery of materials: notice only, full set delivery, or hybrid. Under the "notice only" model, companies must give notice to shareholders indicating the manner in which shareholders can access proxy materials over the Internet at least 40 calendar days before the annual meeting date. Thereafter, instead of sending shareholders paper materials, corporations must post those materials on a generally accessible website. The notice can be sent electronically to any shareholder who previously consented to such delivery. The corporation also must provide a paper copy of the materials to any shareholder who requests them, at no charge. However, a shareholder can make a permanent request to receive her proxy materials in paper or electronically. The initial notice cannot include a proxy card or any other information. The corporation can distribute a proxy card either by email or regular mail ten days after the initial notice. Recent amendments allow corporations to include on the proxy card instructions about the voting process as well as explanations regarding why the corporation has chosen to utilize the notice only option.

Corporations also must enable shareholders to executive their proxies immediately. This means that the corporation must establish a toll-free number for voting, post a proxy card on the website, or establish an electronic voting system.

Alternatively, corporations can choose the "full set delivery" option whereby they deliver all of the proxy materials to shareholders. Companies that rely on the full set delivery option can send the materials in paper form, or electronically as long as shareholders have previously consented to electronic delivery. Companies that choose the full set delivery option do not have to comply with the 40 day rule. Instead, companies comply with the traditional rules governing the dissemination of proxy materials, with two additional requirements. First, companies must post proxy materials on the Internet. Second, companies must include a notice of the electronic availability of proxy materials in their distributed materials, or incorporate the notice in the proxy statement and proxy card.

Finally, corporations can adopt a hybrid method pursuant to which they adopt the notice only model for some shareholders, and a full set delivery option for others.

Shareholders also have the ability to make use of the e-proxy rules. Thus, shareholders can choose to deliver proxy materials pursuant to the notice only model, the full set delivery option, or a hybrid option. In addition, a shareholder—but not a corporation—can limit her solicitation to shareholders who have previously agreed not to request paper copies of proxy materials.

Among other things, the e-proxy rules were designed to reduce the cost associated with dissemination of proxy materials, and thereby facilitate shareholders' ability to nominate and elect directors of their choice or otherwise engage in proxy contests. Many have suggested that one of the primary impediments to shareholders' ability to nominate and elect directors of their choice is the cost associated with waging a proxy contest. Because the e-proxy rules enable shareholders to disseminate materials electronically, they reduce the printing and mailing costs associated with delivering proxy materials. Indeed, some insisted that the e-proxy rules would ameliorate the need to provide shareholders' access to the corporation's proxy statement for purposes of nominating shareholders of their choice.[8]

The available data reveals that corporations who have used the notice only option have saved significant sums of money. Such companies saved some $233 million in 2010.[9]

However, such rules have resulted in significant disenfranchisement of retail shareholders. Thus, evidence reveals a 75% drop in retail shareholder participation after implementation of the e-proxy rules.[10] Importantly, the data reveals a marked difference between retail voting by shareholders who were distributed materials under the notice only option and those who received a full set of documents.[11] With respect to the notice only option, it is clear that many shareholders did not visit the company website where proxy materials were posted, and hence did not cast their vote. This failure may stem from the fact that shareholders were unwilling to take the additional step of visiting the website. It also may stem from shareholder confusion regarding how to access the proxy materials.

The SEC has taken several steps aimed at counteracting this drop in retail participation.[12] The SEC launched a website emphasizing the importance of voting, and pinpointing ways in which shareholders can cast their vote.[13] The SEC also amended the e-proxy rules. Among other things, the amendments enable corporations to provide information about the voting process along with their initial notice to shareholders.

The drop in retail voting is concerning for several reasons. First, and most importantly, it suggests that the e-proxy rules have operated to impede retail shareholders' effective exercise of their vote. Second, it poses challenges for corporations seeking to meet quorum requirements. Third, it magnifies the influence of institutional shareholders, particularly those that are most active.

In light of these concerns, corporations have been reluctant to adopt the notice only model. Instead, corporations either deliver a full set of proxy materials, or adopt a hybrid approach. In either case, corporate reluctance to embrace the notice only model means that such corporations cannot take full advantage of the cost savings associated with e-proxy.

Then too, shareholders have not embraced e-proxy. Data from the 2008 and 2009 proxy seasons revealed that during such seasons, only one shareholder used the notice only model for dissemination of proxy materials.[14] This may stem primarily from the fact that the rules do not have a significant impact on shareholder costs of waging a proxy contests. The costs of printing and mailing proxy materials eliminated by the e-proxy rules are not the only costs involved with proxy solicitations and proxy fights. Instead, the more significant costs stem from legal advice and advertising, costs which are not reduced by electronic delivery of proxy materials. As a result, the rules do not eliminate the sizeable costs that shareholders must incur in connection with a proxy battle. Moreover, the rules could create a competitive disadvantage for shareholders who use a notice only model if adoption of that model leads to a reduction in shareholder voting participation. As this suggests, the e-proxy rules have not had their desired effect.

D. Broker Voting

Many shareholders rely on brokers or other intermediaries to cast their votes for them. For ease of discussion, this chapter will refer to such intermediaries collectively as brokers. It is estimated that as much as 85% of all shares in U.S. public companies are purchased through brokers.[15] When shares are purchased through a broker, the shares are recorded in the broker's name, and held by the broker. Shares held in this fashion are referred to as being held in the "street name." The broker is the record owner of the shares, while shareholders are the beneficial holders of the shares.

As the record holders, brokers—and not shareholders—receive any investor information distributed by the corporation. Brokers have an obligation to provide shareholders with information they receive from the corporation.

Brokers also vote the shares they hold on behalf of the beneficial owners. This means that while the beneficial holders can attend shareholder meetings, they cannot vote their own shares unless they receive a legal proxy from their brokers. Most shareholders do not request such a proxy and hence rely on brokers to cast their votes. In connection with such voting, brokers have an obligation to seek voting instructions from shareholders.

There are some matters on which brokers can vote even when they do not receive instructions from shareholders. New York Stock Exchange Rule 452, adopted in 1937, allows brokers who do not receive instructions from shareholders within 10 days of the scheduled meeting to vote without such instructions.[16] However, such uninstructed or discretionary voting by brokers can only be done with respect to matters that are not considered routine.

Uninstructed voting by brokers raises concerns because brokers overwhelmingly vote in favor of management recommendations. This voting pattern has caused changes in the definition of what constitutes a routine matter. In particular, say on pay votes and uncontested director elections have been removed from the definition of routine matters.

In the 1980s, the SEC implemented rules allowing shareholders who purchase their shares through brokers to elect whether to have contact directly with the company. An objecting beneficial owner, or an "OBO," elects to prohibit the company from directly communicating with her. This means that the shareholder's name and address cannot be disclosed to the corporation. As a result, only the broker may directly contact the shareholder. A non-objecting beneficial owner, or "NOBO," is a shareholder who elects to allow the corporation to engage in direct communication with her. Hence, a company can request a list of NOBOs, which includes shareholders' names, addresses, and ownership positions—but not their email addresses. This OBO/NOBO classification is primarily aimed at protecting the privacy of beneficial owners. A 2006 NYSE Working Group found that some 75% of all retail beneficial owners are OBOs, and that many investors do not understand the distinction between OBOs and NOBOs.[17]

As corporations seek to increase their communications with shareholders, this classification has come into the spotlight because it undermines corporations' ability to directly interact with many of their shareholders. While it is unlikely that the classification will be eliminated entirely, the SEC is considering the best way to ensure that the classification does not unnecessarily impede board-shareholder communication.

E. Empty Voting

Empty voting refers to a situation in which voting power is not connected to economic ownership. The common presumption is that economic ownership is coupled with voting power. However, changes in the manner in which securities are held have challenged this presumption, creating situations of empty voting.

Empty voting can occur in a number of ways. First, shares can be bought and sold between the record date and meeting date. If a shareholder sells her shares after the record date, she may be entitled to vote on matters despite no longer owning the shares. This problem has encouraged corporations to make changes in the record date rules or otherwise close the gap between the meeting date and record date. Second, empty voting can result from share lending, pursuant to which one investor lends her shares to another. The general rule in share lending transactions is that the person who borrows the shares has voting rights, while the person who has loaned the shares has no voting rights. Importantly, beneficial owners are often unaware that their shares have been loaned, and hence are unaware that they cannot vote those shares. In some cases, share lending creates a situation pursuant to which both the borrower and the lender cast their votes, leading to over-voting.

Third, empty voting can arise from reliance on the derivatives market. That market enables people to hedge the economic risk associated with stock ownership by purchasing derivatives. In this regard, derivative markets allow shareholders to obtain voting power with no net economic investment. In some cases, hedging transactions can create a circumstance pursuant to which shareholders have a negative economic interest, potentially giving them an incentive to vote in a manner that reduces a company's value. Then too, hedging transactions may create situations in which shareholders have economic interests that exceed their voting power.

Empty voting has generated considerable concern because it enables shareholders to influence corporate transactions when they have economic interests at odds with the best interest of the corporation. In this regard, there have been a variety of recent transactions in which shareholders have employed empty voting techniques. In response, corporations have sought ways to limit the ability of parities to influence stockholder votes when their economic interests are not coupled with their voting authority.

IV. Shareholder Responsibilities

Traditionally, shareholders have had very few obligations to the corporation or other shareholders. As a general rule, courts impose obligations in two limited settings: (1) when there is a controlling shareholder, and (2) when controlling shareholders use their position to engage in transactions involving a freeze out of minority shareholder interests. A controlling shareholder is generally defined as one who has the ability to direct the affairs of the corporation. While that definition does not require controlling shareholders to hold a majority of the shares, courts only consider shareholders to be controlling if they hold a sizable portion of company stock. Such shareholders owe fiduciary duties to the corporation and other shareholders.

In particular, controlling shareholders have a responsibility in connection with freeze out transactions. A freeze out represents a transaction where controlling shareholders use their influence to cause the corporation to pursue actions that results in minority shareholders being forced to sell their shares. With respect to these transactions, courts have required that controlling shareholders deal fairly with minority shareholders. Outside of these limited settings, shareholders do not have any responsibility to the company or other shareholders.

Some have argued that as shareholders' rights have been enhanced, there should be greater attention to shareholders' responsibility in exercising those rights. Professors Lynn Stout and Iman Anabtawi have argued that shareholders should have a duty of loyalty "triggered whenever a shareholder successfully employs shareholder status to promote corporate actions that gives a person material economic benefit to the detriment or exclusion of other shareholders."[18] However, they recognize that courts may be reluctant to impose additional responsibilities on shareholders in the face of the historically narrow view regarding shareholders' obligations to the corporation and its shareholders.

CHAPTER 3

SHAREHOLDER VOTING: WHY DOES IT MATTER?

I. Shareholder Voting Rights

Shareholders' voting right is often referred to as their most fundamental right. That right is crucial for at least three reasons. First, it serves to legitimize directors' power. The corporation is managed by or under the direction of the board. As a result, directors have considerable discretion to appoint officers who operate the day to day affairs of the corporation, to implement the corporation's business plan and policies, and to determine the corporation's direction. Because shareholders vote directors onto the board, their voting right represents the mechanism through which directors are granted this broad discretion. Therefore, "the shareholder franchise is the ideological underpinning upon which the legitimacy of directorial power rests."[1]

Second, shareholders' ability to remove directors or otherwise refuse to reelect directors operates to discipline corporate officers and directors, ensuring that they pay heed to their fiduciary obligations and do not abuse their discretion. Corporate governance scholars have long recognized that the interests of shareholders and directors are not fully aligned. Thus, without adequate incentives and limits, directors may engage in actions that benefit themselves at the expense of shareholders, or fail to pursue actions that would advance the interests of the corporation and its shareholders. In other words, the corporation produces agency costs. Corporate governance arrangements must be designed to reduce those agency costs, and thus more closely align directors' interests with shareholders'. Shareholders' voting right is intended to serve this purpose. Shareholders' power over directors' fate is supposed to encourage directors to take shareholder interests into account when carrying out their duties.

Third, shareholders' voting power represents their primary means of expressing their concerns within the corporation. Corporate law prohibits shareholders from intervening with most director decisions, particularly those involving the day to day affairs of the corporation. The shareholder vote therefore is one of the few means by which shareholders can communicate their preferences, with the hope that directors will take those preferences into account when making decisions about the corporation. When directors embrace certain policies or practices, shareholders' support (or lack thereof) for such directors helps to convey their preferences about those policies or strategies. The same is true when shareholders vote on proposals or otherwise vote in support of certain policies. In this regard, shareholders' voting right both legitimizes directors' power and serves to ensure that such power is used to advance corporate interests.

II. Comparison to Other Shareholder Rights

Voting is not the only means by which shareholders can express their preferences regarding corporate affairs, or otherwise can encourage managerial accountability. This section discusses some other ways in which shareholders can discipline directors, and compares them with the shareholder vote.

A. Exit or the "Wall Street Rule"

Shareholders have the ability to sell their shares and hence exit the corporation, particularly when the corporation is a public one. This exit right, often referred to as the "Wall Street Rule," has been described as shareholders' ability to "vote with their feet" or to "switch rather than fight." The exit right has at least two important implications for corporate conduct. First, the exit right could serve as a form of disciplining managers because such managers may refrain from engaging in transactions that would prompt significant shareholder exit, particularly when that exit is likely to drive down a company's stock price. Empirical evidence supports the theory that exit or the threat of exit can shape managerial behavior.[2] Second, exit enables shareholders to choose the governance structure they believe to be most appropriate because shareholders can exit one company in favor of another with more appealing policies or procedures. From this perspective, when shareholders exercise their right to exit, it can serve as a form of corporate governance and even shareholder activism.

Exit also may be more beneficial than voting. Exit appears to be a more cost-effective alternative to activism through voting because shareholders do not have to expend resources in order to exit. Exit enables shareholders to seek out corporations with a more appealing governance structure rather than alter a corporation's governance structure in ways that may not be acceptable to other shareholders. Thus, exit may reduce the possibility that a limited group of shareholders imposes their governance agenda on the broader shareholder class.

However, exit has several drawbacks that may make it less appealing than seeking to influence corporate affairs through voting. First, if a company is underperforming, exit may be unappealing because such exit may result in lost profits for the exiting shareholder. Moreover, the very fact that a shareholder exits may drive down stock price, particularly if the shareholder holds a large percentage of shares. As a result, a shareholder's exit may create a situation in which the shareholder will lose money on the sale of stock. Second, given the potential for exit to negatively impact shareholders' ability to recoup or otherwise enhance their investment, voting may be more attractive not only because some forms of shareholder voting are relatively costless, but also because some large shareholders may find it more cost effective to devote the resources necessary to impact governance changes through voting rather than take the stock price hit that may be associated with exiting. Third, exit may not be practical for some corporations. Shareholders with concentrated holdings may find it more difficult to exit because of transaction and other costs associated with selling a large block of shares. It also may be more difficult for diversified shareholders to employ exit because such shareholders must maintain a certain mix of investments. Thus, such shareholders may have limited options when seeking to shift their holdings from one company to another. Fourth, it is possible that exit, particularly by large shareholders, leaves the remaining shareholders worse off. Indeed, large shareholders may have the resources and incentives to be effective monitors. Their exit may leave the remaining shareholders without such monitors, and hence without an important accountability tool. Moreover, a large shareholder's exit may trigger stock declines that negatively impact the remaining shareholders. In these ways, exit may prove less appealing than voting.

B. The Disciplining Effects of Litigation

Shareholders can rely on litigation as a means of shaping corporate conduct. Corporate directors and officers have a fiduciary duty to act in the best interests of the corporation and its shareholders. Shareholders are essentially the only group who can bring suit against directors and officers for breaching this duty. Shareholders also can bring suit against directors and officers when they engage in certain violations of the federal securities laws. Presumably this ability to bring such suits has an impact on director and officer conduct because directors and officers seeking to avoid such suits will engage in behavior that advances the interests of the corporation and shareholders. Litigation, therefore, is an important tool for reducing agency costs and aligning the interests of shareholders and managers.

However, litigation may be a very difficult tool to wield because of the procedural and substantive hurdles associated with bringing a lawsuit. With respect to shareholder derivative suits under state law, procedural hurdles, such as the requirement of making a demand on the corporation and the ability of special litigation committees to dismiss suits before trial, undermine shareholders' ability to bring actions against directors. Even if shareholders overcome such procedural hurdles, the deference granted to director decisions makes it exceedingly difficult to hold directors accountable for all but the most egregious offenses. Empirical studies reveal only a handful of cases in which directors have been held liable for breaching their fiduciary duty of care.[3] Moreover, even after a director is found liable, indemnification, insurance, and exculpatory charter provisions combine to ensure that directors rarely incur out of pocket damages for such liability. Empirical evidence confirms that such provisions result in almost no outside director being held personally liable for breaching their fiduciary duties.[4] Shareholders experience similar difficulties in connection with federal securities actions. That is, procedural rules such as heightened pleading requirements, as well as substantive rules, make it difficult for shareholders to successfully bring actions against directors. In this regard, researchers have concluded that the risk of personal liability for directors, particularly outside directors, is relatively low.[5]

Nonetheless, some argue that shareholders' ability to bring litigation impacts directors' decision-making. Even if shareholder suits are not successful, directors and officers seek to avoid shareholders lawsuits, including the reputational sanctions they may incur as a result of such suits. Thus, the threat of lawsuit serves to impact corporate conduct in a way that could alter or improve managerial behavior.

However, the difficulties associated with litigation as a remedy coupled with timing and cost considerations may make it less attractive than voting. Indeed, litigation involves significant time. For example, when shareholders brought a derivative action against Disney directors alleging a breach of their duties, it took eight years to resolve—and the shareholders were ultimately unsuccessful in holding such directors liable. By contrast, shareholders' voting campaign resulted in governance changes at Disney within a very short period of time. Those changes included prompting Disney's board chair to step down and getting the company to implement majority voting within months after their campaign on this issue. In addition to these timing concerns, litigation can be costly. While some shareholder voting efforts involve significant cost, there are others that are relatively costless and thus may be a better alternative than litigation.

At the very least, the shortcomings associated with litigation may mean that it cannot serve as shareholders' exclusive method for influencing corporate affairs. Consistent with this observation, many shareholders that actively participate in shareholder suits, including serving as lead plaintiffs in those suits, also routinely rely on voting campaigns to influence corporate governance.

C. The Market for Corporate Control

Some believe that the market for corporate control—that is, the market for takeovers—creates a strong incentive for corporate officers and directors to act responsibly. If managers fail to efficiently operate the company, the company's shares will drop, making the company an easy target for those seeking to purchase control of the company and potentially replace incumbent directors and officers with a team that will act to maximize the company's value. From this perspective, the market for corporate control ensures that directors and officers do not ignore opportunities that will increase shareholder value. Indeed, the fact that shareholders are required to vote in connection with change of control transactions enhances the impact of the market for corporate control because it ensures that shareholders can influence the outcome of such transactions. The market for corporate control therefore decreases the likelihood of managers furthering their own interests at the expense of shareholder value, and thus serves as a mechanism for influencing corporate governance.

However, empirical evidence undermines the theory that takeovers necessarily focus on the worst managed companies and hence serve as a mechanism for improving performance.[6] Instead, some studies reveal that bidders are equally as likely to target a well-performing company as one that is under-performing. Other studies indicate that bidders are not motivated by a perceived inefficiency of the target's management team, and instead actively seek out companies with strong management teams. Still others reveal that incumbent managers often remain at a company post-takeover. If takeovers do not focus on poorly managed companies, it is not clear that they serve to incentivize managers of such companies to engage in value-enhancing activities. As a result, the discipline impact of the takeover market may be uneven at best.[7]

Moreover, the disciplining impact of the corporate control market, to the extent it exists, may be limited to companies at which there is gross under-performance. Takeover artists must pay a sizable premium over the existing stock price. A rational bidder will only offer such a premium when there is a strong possibility of significant future value following the takeover. As a result, managements' conduct must have a considerable impact on stock performance before their conduct would attract the attention of a hostile bidder. There may be many instances of director and officer misconduct that do not result in a significant enough stock price decline to attract the attention of those who would seek to obtain control of a company. As a result, this market may only impact corporate conduct in egregious instances, and hence may not be an effective accountability measure.[8]

Engaging in takeovers also involves significant costs, which include the cost of waging a takeover battle as well as the cost associated with ferreting out information about mismanagement. The costs associated with such actions may undermine their effectiveness because only when takeovers warrant the costs will they be conducted. Moreover, such costs may make them less viable than other voting mechanisms that may be less costly.

III. The Shareholder Democracy Debate

Shareholders' efforts to increase their voting rights over corporate affairs has sparked intense debate. Notably, a 2005 edition of the *Harvard Law Review* featured advocates on both sides of this debate. In his article, *The Case for Increasing Shareholder Power*, Professor Lucian Bebchuk, one of the leading proponents of enhancing shareholder power, argued that increasing shareholder power would improve corporate governance and enhance shareholder value.[9] Professor Bebchuk not only supports shareholder efforts to enhance the effectiveness of their existing voting power, but also proposes a regime that would enable shareholders to initiate and adopt changes related to the corporation's basic governance arrangements. Professor Bebchuk insists that enabling shareholders to adopt what he calls "rules-of-the-game" decisions will directly and indirectly improve corporate decision-making, and will better align that decision-making with shareholder interests. Critics of enhancing shareholder power, particularly Professor Stephen Bainbridge, disagree.[10] Such critics contend that increasing shareholder power undermines the primary benefit of the corporate form, centralized decision-making, and thus undermines the ability of corporations to operate in the most effective and efficient manner. Critics also maintain that increasing shareholder power not only could undermine corporate value, but could also enable some shareholders to advance their own personal agendas at the expense of other shareholders and the corporation as a whole.

This section pinpoints some of the primary arguments surrounding the cases for and against increased shareholder power. But first, this section examines the debate surrounding use of the term "shareholder democracy."

A. The Democracy Debate and What's in a Name

Because shareholders' recent engagement centers on their desire to make their voting power more effective, that engagement has been referred to as "shareholder democracy." Such a reference captures the notion that shareholders participate in the corporation through voting, as well as the notion that director decisions should reflect or represent shareholder concerns. In other words, the bid for shareholder democracy reflects a bid for the corporation to be more representative and participatory by allowing shareholders to exercise greater voice within the corporation.

Importantly, referring to shareholder activism as democracy has strategic advantages for activists. Indeed, such a reference makes the activist campaign more accessible by encouraging people to draw parallels between shareholders' plight and democratic principles surrounding the importance of the vote. It also generates strong support for the campaign by appealing to America's basic preference in favor of democratic regimes. An *Economist* article captures the power of this appeal: "America is the world's most prominent democracy, and its most successful exponent of shareholder capitalism. But when it comes to shareholder democracy America has barely moved beyond the corporate equivalent of the rotten borough."[11] Put in those terms, who could be against shareholder democracy?

Critics insist that the term "democracy" is a misnomer as applied to the corporation. In their view, the corporation is not a form of participatory democracy. Instead, the corporation is designed to ensure that shareholders have limited opportunities to participate in the corporation, while directors have broad discretion to engage in actions that they believe to be in the best interests of the corporation. Moreover, the corporation is not a form of representative democracy. That is, directors' and officers' actions are not intended to exclusively represent the interests of shareholders. Instead, corporate directors and officers have a duty to advance the interest of the corporate enterprise, which includes paying heed to the concerns of the many stakeholders within that enterprise. Consequently, critics insist that seeking to construe shareholder activism as a form of democracy is inappropriate.

Nevertheless, many refer to shareholder activism in this area as shareholder democracy. While some of that reference may be strategic, proponents also believe that the term appropriately encompasses the notion that shareholders are seeking to ensure that their voting power is effective, and that directors must (at least at some level) act as their representatives.[12]

B. The Case for Increased Shareholder Power

Proponents offer several reasons for enhancing shareholder power. First, increasing shareholder power facilitates shareholders' ability to exercise their state law voting right. Indeed, in many situations legal and practical hurdles make it difficult for shareholders to exercise their voting rights in elections or to use their vote to communicate with the corporation. Much of the campaign to increase shareholder power focuses on removing obstacles to shareholders' existing rights. As a result, increasing shareholder power is appropriate because it only aims to ensure that shareholders can exercise their existing rights more effectively and efficiently.

Second, increasing shareholder power enables shareholders to play a critical role in holding directors accountable for their actions. Giving shareholders greater voting power, particularly with respect to director elections, ensures that directors' interests are more closely aligned with shareholder's interests. As a result, increasing shareholder power helps prevent shirking and mismanagement by giving directors strong incentives to advance the corporate interests and avoid self-dealing.

Third, increasing shareholder power reduces the need to rely on outside regulators and legislators. In other words, if shareholders can monitor the corporation and serve as a check on corporate misconduct, their actions reduce the need for regulation. Shareholder power then serves as a form of self-regulation. Recent federal regulations that grant shareholders enhanced power seem to explicitly rely on the notion that such power operates as an accountability measure that may reduce the need for governmental intervention in corporate affairs.

Fourth, increasing shareholder power increases the likelihood that directors and officers will adopt value-enhancing policies. Shareholders are incentivized to pursue policies that maximize the corporation's value. Thus, increasing shareholders' power also increases their ability to influence corporate decision-making in a way that augments value. Professor Bebchuk argues that the campaign for increasing shareholder power should move beyond merely enhancing shareholder rights within the existing governance regime, and instead should seek to give shareholders the ability to initiate "rules of the game" decisions such as amending the charter or determining the state of incorporation. Granting shareholders' power over those decisions will better ensure that directors adopt value-maximizing governance arrangements.

Recent evidence reveals that shareholders can use their voting rights to alter the governance structure of corporations. While shareholder activism historically did not yield success, this recent wave has been different. Shareholders have managed to alter the standard by which directors are elected, as well as the nature of the terms directors serve. Shareholder activism has also resulted in them having a greater voice in certain decisions, including decisions over executive compensation. Shareholders have waged election battles that not only have resulted in board changes, but also have altered the direction of the targeted corporation. Finally, for decades shareholders have sought to gain access to the corporation's proxy statement for purposes of nominating director candidates of their choice. And these efforts have finally resulted in the SEC passing proxy access rules for the first time in history.

Finally, some recent empirical evidence suggests that increased shareholder power improves corporate performance. Recent studies not only reveal that the market reacts favorably to shareholder activism, but also that, overall, such activism has resulted in improved performance at the targeted companies.[13] Such studies focus on activism by hedge funds, which specifically target companies with low market value and aim to improve their profitability. Studies reveal that the increased stock performance is most positive when such funds focus on changes in business strategy rather than changes in a company's capital structure. Because hedge fund activism is a relatively recent phenomenon, it is not clear how reliable such studies are with respect to long-term value, nor is it clear that research involving the impact of hedge fund activism can be applicable to the broader shareholder class. Nevertheless, the research provides some support for the proposition that shareholder activism enhances corporate value, and thus can be beneficial.

C. The Case against Increased Shareholder Power

Like proponents of shareholder power, critics advance several reasons why increasing shareholder power is not appropriate. First, it is possible that shareholders will not take advantage of their increased power, which could prove especially problematic if such power is deemed a substitute for outside regulation or other forms of accountability measures. The conventional wisdom is that shareholders are rationally apathetic. Shareholder voting is fraught with free-rider and collective action problems that decrease the likelihood that shareholders will exercise their vote. As a result, increasing shareholder power will have little to no impact on corporate governance because shareholders will not have incentives to use their power. Moreover, increasing shareholder power does not avoid the need for better or more efficient outside regulation.

Second, even if shareholders use their increased power, that use will not be effective because shareholders lack the expertise and information necessary to make efficient business decisions. From this perspective, there is no guarantee that shareholders will have the requisite qualifications to make informed business decisions. Then too, shareholders are at an informational disadvantage vis-à-vis directors and officers who are better informed about the web of financial and business issues impacting the corporation. This undermines the extent to which placing power in the hands of shareholders will result in better decision-making.

Third, increasing shareholder power will increase the ability of some shareholders to advance their own personal agendas, potentially to the detriment of the broader shareholder class. Some shareholders' actions could lead to green mail pursuant to which corporate managers will attempt to buy off shareholders engaged in activism. Other shareholders may have the ability to force the corporation to pursue actions that do not benefit all shareholders. This may be especially true for shareholders who are only interested in short-term profit as opposed to the long-term health of the corporation. In fact, there is some empirical evidence suggesting that some shareholders use their voting rights as a tool for advancing their own special interests. The possibility that increased shareholder power will be used in this manner makes such increased power unattractive.

Importantly, the fact that shareholders have competing interests enhances the possibility that shareholder empowerment will lead to shareholders advancing their own personal agenda. Professor Iman Anabtawi argues that the shareholder power debate fails to sufficiently appreciate the divergent interests of shareholders. Some have short-term interests, while others are focused on the long run. Some have diversified interests, while others have their shares tied up with one company. In light of these varying interests, shifting power to shareholders would encourage rent-seeking whereby shareholders would use their influence to extract private benefits that impose costs on other shareholders. Increasing shareholder power also would encourage inter-shareholder fighting in ways that would be counterproductive to the corporation's overall health.[14]

Fourth, increasing shareholder power may undermine the corporation's ability to attend to the interests of non-shareholder stakeholders. Professors Margaret Blair and Lynn Stout have suggested that the corporate board serves as a mediator of various interests within the corporation.[15] Shifting power to shareholders undermines this mediating role, and hence undermines the board's ability and willingness to advance these other interests effectively. Instead, increased shareholder power could force directors and officers to focus on shareholders to the detriment of other stakeholders.[16]

Then too, increasing shareholder power undermines the efficiency of the corporate form. Establishing a system of corporate governance requires determining how best to allocate the decision rights within the corporation. A centralized management system ensures that corporate managers are better positioned to make decisions more quickly, efficiently, and at a lower cost than shareholders. Such managers also have greater knowledge and experience with operating the day to day affairs of the company, giving them an enhanced ability to make decisions about those affairs. Thus, it is neither feasible nor desirable to have shareholders make the day to day decisions in the corporation. Instead, the most preferable regime is one in which shareholders and other corporate stakeholders delegate the decision-making authority to the board and officers. In this regard, Professor Bainbridge argues that increased shareholder power would undermine one of the benefits of the American corporation because the most effective and efficient method of managing a large corporation is to delegate authority to a central decision-making body, while providing limited rights for shareholders.[17]

Consistent with this observation, empirical studies suggest that most shareholders prefer a corporate regime of limited shareholder power. Those studies reveal that when corporations go public, and shareholders have to make a choice about the governance regime they will select, they choose a system with weak shareholder rights. Hence, as Professor Stout points out, when shareholders have a preference regarding corporate governance rules, they opt into those rules that strengthen director power and ensure that shareholders have more limited power.[18] This data weakens the case for shareholder power, and suggests that the shareholder empowerment movement may be the result of activism by a small group of shareholders.

Empirical studies also suggest that increasing shareholder power has little impact on corporate stock price or corporate performance.[19] Indeed, several studies have evaluated the impact of shareholder proposals and private negotiations between shareholders and management on corporate performance in the short or the long term. When viewed together, those studies indicate that while such forms of shareholder activism may lead to changes in the targeted company's governance procedures, they have no significant impact on stock performance or corporate earnings.[20]

D. Debating the Debate

How does one resolve this debate? First, while it may be true that some shareholders will not exercise their voting power if it is enhanced, such an observation may suggest why increased shareholder power cannot be the exclusive form of managerial accountability, but does not necessarily undermine the case for increased shareholder power. Then too, it is clear that some shareholders are willing to engage in activism, and hence that some shareholders are likely to use any increased power.

Second, it seems relatively clear that some shareholders may not be well-informed, while others may only be interested in using their voting power solely for the purpose of advancing their own personal agenda. One response to such a criticism may be that shareholders need the support of a majority of the shareholder class in order to directly implement any corporate changes. This need undermines the extent to which shareholders can be successful in advancing their own narrow personal interest. However, this response is not fully satisfying because shareholders can influence the corporation indirectly even without majority support, either by encouraging green mail or by encouraging corporate managers to concede to their demands in order to avoid costly activist campaigns. Consequently, increased shareholder power inevitably increases the possibility that some shareholders will use their power in ways that could negatively impact the corporation as a whole.

Third, it also seems possible that advancing shareholder interests could lead directors to neglect non-shareholder interests. Importantly, however, at least some evidence not only suggests that shareholders support non-shareholder concerns, but also that shareholders have sought to advance those concerns even as they increase their activism around corporate governance issues.[21] This is especially true for shareholders who appreciate that the long-term health of the corporation is dependent on addressing the needs of all stakeholders.

Finally, the empirical evidence tells two different stories. To be sure, advancing shareholder power has had an impact on corporate governance structures, but it is not clear if that impact translates into improved corporate performance. More recent campaigns suggest that increased shareholder power can have positive repercussions for corporate performance, but it is not clear how reliable such data is with respect to all shareholders or if it will continue to be true for the long term.

Viewed together, both sides of this debate make compelling arguments. Of course, regardless of the propriety of shareholder power, the reality is that shareholders have begun to play a greater role in shaping the corporate governance landscape. As a result, debating the merits of shareholder empowerment may be moot. Instead, it may be more important to gain a better understanding of shareholders' increased role, so that we can better understand, and prepare for, what that role will mean for the corporation and future governance issues. The remainder of this book is dedicated to providing such an understanding.

CHAPTER 4

THE EVOLVING SHAREHOLDER LANDSCAPE AND ITS IMPACT ON SHAREHOLDER ENGAGEMENT

The shareholder landscape has undergone tremendous changes over the last few decades. The current increase in shareholder activism cannot be appreciated without understanding those changes. This chapter discusses such changes, the kinds of shareholders that engage in activism, and the role of shareholders or proxy advisor services in that engagement.

I. The Evolving Shareholder Landscape

Much of the story about the changing shareholder landscape centers around the decline of individual or so-called retail investors, and the corresponding increase in the amount of securities held by institutional investors—a category that includes banks, public and private pension funds, investment companies (including mutual funds and closed-end funds), insurance companies, broker, and dealers. The shift towards increased institutional share ownership of the U.S. equity securities market, coupled with the change in the type of institutional shareholders participating in the market, has played a significant role in the new shareholder environment.

A. The Decline of the Retail Investor

Historically, individuals owned the vast majority of U.S. equity securities. In 1950, individual investors held about 90% of the U.S.

equity market.[1] In 1970, the percentage of stock held by individuals had fallen to 78%.[2] In 1990, individual investors accounted for 56% of the U.S. equity market.[3] By 2009, such investors' share ownership had declined even further. Thus, individual investors currently own approximately 36% of the U.S. equity market.[4] This ownership level stands in sharp contrast to their near domination of that market in 1950.

B. The Rise of the Institutional Investor

1. Institutional Shareholder Dominance

In comparison to retail investors, institutional investors have played an increasingly greater role in the U.S. equity market. In 1950, institutional investors only held about 6% of the U.S. equity market.[5] In 1970, institutional ownership had climbed to 18%,[6] and by 1990 such ownership reached about 37%.[7] Federal Reserve figures indicate that institutional ownership accounted for approximately 50% of the equity market in 2009.[8] Other figures reflect institutional ownership levels as high as 66%.[9] In either case, such figures clearly reveal that institutional investors account for a significant sector of the equity securities market.

Importantly, such figures may not accurately reflect institutional investor dominance for at least two reasons. First, hedge funds are not required to provide information related to their assets. Thus, the Federal Reserve date does not separately account for securities held by hedge funds.[10] Instead, securities held by hedge funds are included in the data associated with individual ownership.[11] This inclusion distorts the share ownership picture, suggesting that the percentage of individual ownership is less than the data reveals while the percentage of institutional ownership is greater. Given the rapid growth of hedge funds and their tendency to engage in shareholder activism, this distortion is especially significant.

The second reason why the available data may not fully reflect institutional shareholder dominance is that institutional ownership is significantly higher at the largest American corporations. In 1990, institutional investors held roughly 49% of the equity securities at the 1,000 largest U.S. companies.[12] In 2007, institutional ownership at such companies reached a historical high of 76.4%.[13] Despite the recession and corresponding declines in institutional equity holdings, institutional investors continue to own sizeable chunks of the nation's largest companies. Thus, in 2009, institutions held 73% of the equity securities at the 1,000 largest U.S. companies.[14]

Institutional holdings vary significantly by company. Companies like Google and Wells Fargo stand out because of their sizeable institutional ownership. Institutions hold 76% of Google shares and 75% of Wells Fargo shares.[15] By contrast, only 49% of General Electric shares and 35% of Wal-Mart shares are in the hands of institutions.[16] Despite this variance, these figures reveal that institutions have a significant presence in the top American companies.

The rise in institutional holdings has repercussions for shareholder activism because such institutions have the resources, expertise, and incentive-structures that make them more likely to engage in activism.

2. Changes in the Balance of Power among Institutions

There also has been a shift in the type of institutions holding equity securities. Mutual funds have expanded their presence in this market. In 1980, mutual funds held only 2.5% of the total institutional shareholder assets.[17] By 2009, this percentage had escalated to 27.4%.[18] This growth in the proportion of assets held by mutual funds has a direct impact on shareholder activism because mutual funds tend to be more active than private pension funds.

Hedge funds have grown exponentially within the last two decades. The lack of regulation over hedge funds makes it difficult to determine precisely what proportion of the equity market they control. However, in 2009, hedge funds controlled more than $1.6 trillion of assets, a portion of which is attributable to equity securities.[19]

Moreover, other institutions invest in hedge funds, increasing hedge funds' reach and impact. In 2009, pension funds invested 13.2% of their holdings in hedge funds and alternative holdings, while investment companies invested 9.6% of their holdings in such entities.[20] Some pension funds have invested more than 20% of their assets into hedge funds.[21] The institutional investment in hedge funds contributes to the growth and influence of such entities, generating a shareholder class distinctly different from the shareholders of 1950.

C. The "New" Shareholders' Impact on Activism

The changed composition of the shareholder class has repercussions for shareholders in terms of their willingness and ability to engage in activism. The amount and concentration of institutional share ownership increases the potential that institutions can overcome the collective action problems associated with individual owners. First, their ownership pattern increases their ability to communicate not only with the corporation and its managers, but also with other institutions, thereby enhancing their ability to impact corporate affairs. Indeed, a relatively small universe of institutions accounts for the equity ownership in the top companies, enhancing their ability to communicate across corporations. Second, such a universe makes it easier for institutions to coordinate their activities across major companies in a manner that influences corporate governance at particular companies and within the corporate community more generally. Moreover, institutions are diversified and thus own securities at a variety of different companies, which also enables them to impact changes across the corporate spectrum. Finally, the size of institutional ownership coupled with the diversification of that ownership means that efforts to influence a corporation's affairs may be a better option than exiting from the corporation. In these ways, institutional shareholders are better positioned to play an active role in corporate governance. Hence, their increased presence in the corporate shareholder base greatly explains the expanded role that shareholders have played in the corporate arena.

Of course, not every institution engages in activism, and even those that do engage do not participate in the same way and at the same rate. The next section examines the roles various shareholders have played in seeking to influence corporate affairs.

II. Activist Shareholders

As institutions gained greater prominence in the equity market, many people believed that they had characteristics that not only would make it especially likely for them to take an active role in overseeing corporate affairs, but also would insure that their oversight would have a positive impact on these affairs. On the one hand, in addition to their ability to coordinate their efforts and communicate with other institutions, their diversification meant that they would focus on universal issues impacting the market as a whole. Then too, because such institutions had no connection with management, it was believed that their oversight would not involve the kinds of conflicts of interests that could undermine the objectivity of some directors. It was also believed that many institutions had incentives to focus on the long term, particularly pension funds whose investments focused on safe-guarding retirement assets. In these ways, institutions appeared ideally situated to use their influence to monitor corporate affairs and hold corporations accountable for any mismanagement of those affairs.

However, it became evident that institutions faced hurdles that not only undermined their ability to engage in activism, but also raised questions about the efficacy of that activism. In fact, many institutions continue to play a relatively passive role in the corporate arena. Others have been more active, but their activism has generated concerns about conflicts of interest as well as about the impact of political or other pressures that may limit the extent to which such shareholders' activism benefits the corporation and the broader shareholder class.

This section discusses some of the shareholders who have engaged in activism, as well as the benefits and drawbacks that their activism may create.

A. Pension Funds

For several decades, pension funds have controlled the largest block of institutional assets. In 1980, pension funds controlled about 35% of the total institutional assets.[22] Two decades later, their share of such assets is virtually the same at 39%.[23] However, the type of pension funds that account for such asset holdings has changed over time. Holdings by private pension funds—those managed by corporations or other entities—have declined, while holdings by public pension funds, those managed by state or local governments, have increased. While private pension funds do not have a tendency to engage in activism, public pension funds represent some of the most active institutional investors in the corporate arena.

The largest and by far the most active U.S. public pension fund is the California Public Employees Pension System ("CalPERS"). Although created in 1987, CalPERS did not turn to activism until 1992. CalPERS' activism takes several forms, including:

- Identifying underperforming companies with poor governance practices, and then pressing for changes in those practices.
- Taking an active role in sponsoring or participating in the shareholder proposal process.
- Engaging in withhold the vote campaigns.
- Engaging in securities fraud actions against corporate officers and directors, including serving as lead plaintiff in such actions.
- Publishing a yearly "focus" list of corporations with especially poor governance practices.

Recent studies indicate that while CalPERS has played a dominant role in shareholder activism, there is significantly less engagement by other public pension funds.[24] As an initial matter, public pension funds with the most assets under management also tend to be the most active, while other funds have very little involvement in activism. When funds do engage in activism, they engage in a narrow range of low-visibility endeavors. Thus, outside of CalPERS, when public pension funds engage in activism, the activities they are most likely to participate in are withhold the vote campaigns, writing or signing comment letters to the SEC, and communicating with other investors.[25] Fewer than 20% submit shareholder proposals, and fewer than 15% submit or even suggest director nominees to the board.[26] Importantly, available data indicates that no fund has ever nominated a director to the board.[27] Such funds do tend to participate in shareholder litigation, in many cases serving as lead plaintiffs. However, this data suggests that outside of CalPERS and litigation-related actions, most public pension funds are passive investors.

Several factors limit the ability of public pension funds to engage in activism. The first is cost. Most public pension funds do not have a budget for engaging in corporate governance activities. Hence, most public pension fund activism centers around low-cost activities. Second, most funds do not have the resources or expertise necessary to identify and target particular underperforming companies or problematic governance practices. CalPERS has an investment staff dedicated to gaining such expertise. Thus, to the extent these other funds engage in activism, such funds heavily rely on CalPERS or outside advisors to gain relevant information about a company's performance and governance apparatus. As a result, at best, most other funds simply follow CalPERS' lead. Third, some funds shy away from active engagement because of the negative perception surrounding such engagement.

Indeed, some studies suggest that public pension funds are subject to political pressure that may cause them to engage in campaigns that do not benefit the corporation and its other shareholders. One survey of public pension fund activism indicated that political pressure from government officials may dictate the type of investments funds make as well as the kinds of governance policies they pursue.[28] Such pressure may create conflicts of interest between public pension funds and other shareholders because such funds may be compelled to pursue objectives that are inconsistent with the interests of other shareholders. These studies contribute to the negative perception of public pension fund activism that causes some funds to steer clear of active engagement.

B. Labor Unions and Affiliated Funds

Labor unions also have played an active role in the shareholder landscape. Such unions often exert influence through the equity positions they hold in union pension funds. Since the 1990s, labor unions have been some of the most aggressive institutional shareholders. Such unions not only have been active users of the shareholder proposal process, but also have been active participants in withhold the vote campaigns. In fact, in many years, labor unions are responsible for submitting more than 50% of the shareholders governance proposals. Labor unions also are one of the few institutions that attend annual meetings in order to introduce proposals from the floor of the meeting.

Two entities that have played a prominent role in labor union activism have been the AFL-CIO, the largest federation of unions in the United States, and American Federation of State, County and Municipal Employees ("AFSCME"), the largest union in the AFL-CIO. Both of these entities play an active role in the corporate governance arena, with particular emphasis on submitting shareholder proposals and engaging in withhold the vote campaigns.

Labor union activism has generated significant concern. Some studies indicate that labor unions target companies that are actively engaged in contract negations with union workers, and hence that such activism reflects part of a campaign to win concessions for such workers.[29] Importantly, that research suggests that conflicts of interest between labor union objectives and shareholder interests mean that often labor unions engage in activism to benefit workers at the expense of shareholders.[30] However, other researchers, while acknowledging that some labor union activism aims to advance the interest of workers at the expense of shareholders, nevertheless conclude that most of the activism pursued by labor unions benefits the corporation as a whole.[31] In response to allegations regarding its voting behavior, AFL-CIO published documents emphasizing the notion that its voting policies were aimed at ensuring that any votes it cast were not influenced by conflicts of interest, and thus unconnected with the union status of a company's employees.[32]

C. Mutual Funds

Mutual funds are entities that pool investor funds and invest those funds in a variety of different securities. Mutual funds are regulated under the Investment Company Act, which imposes several requirements on such funds, including dictating the type of fees they can charge, and mandating that such funds maintain diverse portfolios. Mutual funds are the investment vehicle of choice for many investors because they offer individuals an opportunity to invest in a diverse portfolio of securities.

Historically, mutual funds avoided activism, and their voting tended to closely follow management recommendation. Mutual funds cannot accumulate large stakes in a company, nor can they pay managers the type of compensation that might incentivize them to aggressively engage in activism. Mutual funds also do not have the ability to divert significant resources to engaging in activism. As a result, such funds tended to be relatively passive investors.

More recently, mutual fund activism has been on the rise.[33] Such funds have actively participated, and even taken the lead in, takeover battles and other corporate control transactions. Mutual funds also have increasingly cooperated with other institutions to support governance changes. Thus, mutual funds not only have supported and even sponsored shareholder governance proposals related to majority voting and abolishing classified boards, but also have actively supported various withhold the vote campaigns. Importantly, mutual funds have worked together with hedge funds to support their agenda at particular companies. Some believe that increased mutual fund activism can be attributed to the 2003 SEC rule change requiring mutual funds to disclose their voting behavior, and mutual funds' desire to demonstrate their independence as well as their ability to effectively monitor corporate directors and officers.

D. Hedge Funds

Hedge funds have risen to prominence in the last few years because of their high profile activist campaigns, the relative success of those campaigns, and the controversy surrounding their actions.

There is no clear definition of what constitutes a hedge fund. Instead, they are best defined by a set of common characteristics.

First, they are pooled investment vehicles that invest primarily in public securities that place restrictions on the type of investors who can participate in the hedge fund. Second, they are structured to ensure that they will be exempt from most federal regulation. Such funds restrict investment to high net worth individuals or institutions so that they can avoid application of the federal securities laws requiring disclosure about the fund and its activities. They also limit the number of investors within the fund to avoid being subject to regulation under the Investment Company Act. Hedge funds therefore manage to avoid being regulated under most federal securities laws other than the anti-fraud provisions of such laws. Hedge funds' avoidance of such regulation plays an important role in their ability to aggressively engage in activism.

Third, hedge funds are organized by a professional investment manager who not only has a significant stake in the fund she manages, but also receives a relatively high performance-based management fee. This distinguishes hedge funds from both mutual funds and pension funds. Mutual funds cannot charge such amounts because the Investment Company Act limits the types of fees entities can charge. State law and political pressures limit pension funds' ability to charge such fees. Hedge funds' ability to create compensation structures linked to performance contributes to the hedge fund managers' willingness to engage in activism.

Fourth, hedge funds pursue investment and financial strategies unavailable to other entities. Hedge funds concentrate their holdings in a particular company, which other funds cannot do because the Investment Company Act requires that funds maintain a diversified portfolio. Hedge funds also can require investors to lock up their funds for a specified period of time, as long as two or three years. This ensures that hedge fund managers have a relatively illiquid pool of assets with which they can invest. Because the Investment Company Act requires regulated entities like mutual funds to allow investors to sell their shares more frequently, those funds do not have the same kind of access to investor funds. Hedge funds also can engage in margin and derivatives trading; federal law prohibits other institutions from engaging in such trading. In this regard, hedge funds' lack of regulatory restraint distinguishes them from other institutions, while further facilitating their ability to adopt strategies that enable them to engage in activism.

Importantly, most hedge funds do not engage in activism. One estimate indicates that only about 5% of hedge fund assets are used for activism.[34] Thus, the vast majority of hedge funds are not involved in shareholder activism.

However, hedge funds that do so engage have captured the attention of the corporate governance community. Unlike other institutions, hedge fund activism is proactive. Other institutions use their investment power to push for improvement at companies in which they already own shares. By contrast, hedge funds actively seek out underperforming companies with the potential for significant improvement and then engage in an array of tactics aimed at enhancing corporate performance. Hence, hedge funds may pressure corporations to adopt policies aimed at returning value to shareholders, or otherwise pursue transactions aimed at enhancing shareholder value. Hedge funds also seek board representation either through direct negotiations with the corporation or by waging proxy contests. Hedge funds actively support withhold the vote campaigns as well as shareholder proposals, particularly those aimed at dismantling anti-takeover policies, such as proposals to declassify the board, facilitate shareholders' ability to call special meetings, or remove poison pills.

Studies suggest that hedge fund activism involves a high degree of coordination with other institutions. Indeed, part of the hedge fund strategy is to target corporations with a large institutional shareholder base and then collaborate with pension funds, mutual funds, and other entities to influence corporate affairs. Hedge funds also work with other hedge funds. It is often the case that when a hedge fund focuses on a particular company, other hedge funds join in their campaign. This collaboration is referred to as a "wolf pack," and has been the subject of concern because it appears to reflect concerted, but undisclosed, actions among hedge funds in violation of the federal securities law requirement that actions taken in collaboration be disclosed as such.

Hedge fund activism has been very successful. Empirical evidence reveals that, historically, institutional activism has only led to small changes in corporate governance structures.[35] By contrast, according to one study, hedge funds have experienced success or partial success in nearly two-thirds of their campaigns.[36]

Hedge funds are able to achieve success because of their organizational and compensation structure. First, their compensation structure enables them to employ managers who are extremely incentivized. Second, their lack of regulation not only enables them to hold highly concentrated ownership positions, but also enables them to use leverage and derivatives to enhance their holdings. Third, hedge funds do not have significant conflicts of interest with managers in whose companies they hold shares.

Hedge funds have been deeply criticized. Likely the most significant criticism is that they have a short-term focus that causes them to pursue policies that do not benefit the long-term interest of a company. At least one study suggests that hedge funds are not necessarily short-term in focus.[37] Instead, on average, hedge funds hold securities for at least a year, while some hold them for at least as long as twenty months. These holding patterns actually appear longer than some mutual funds that may have more frequent turnover rates. Regardless, some hedge funds do appear to have short-term horizons that call into question the extent to which their actions benefit the long-term health of the corporation. Second, there is concern about the voting behavior of hedge funds. Hedge funds' use of derivatives and other financial innovations enables them to vote shares in a company even when they do not have an economic interest in the company or when they may have an incentive to act in ways that are not in the best interest of a targeted company. While empty voting techniques are not unique to hedge funds, such entities have the ability to exploit those techniques in ways that are not available to other entities that are constrained by federal and other regulations.

Hedge funds' use of such tactics generated a lawsuit in 2008. In the case, CSX Corporation ("CSX") filed a complaint against the Children's Investment Fund ("TCI") and 3G Capital Partners ("3G"), two hedge funds who were engaged in a proxy contest with CSX, for failing to disclose their beneficial ownership of CSX, as required by Section 13(d) of the Exchange Act.[38] Section 13(d) requires entities to file a Schedule 13(d) with the SEC whenever they acquire more than 5% of a company's securities. The purpose of such a filing is to give companies and shareholders advance warning about shareholders intentions, particularly their intentions to seek control of the company.

The case focused on two key issues. The first centered around the extent to which derivative transactions such as equity swaps should be used to calculate beneficial ownership. Both hedge funds had engaged in equity swap transactions associated with CSX stock whereby they had economic interests in the stock, but no voting rights. However, the court reasoned that the counterparty in such transactions could decide to purchase or sell CSX stock in order to cover the swap. Thus, while the court recognized that the hedge funds had no direct voting rights in the stock, it nevertheless concluded that the swap transactions should be used to calculate their beneficial ownership because the counterparty would be likely to vote shares in a manner that would benefit the hedge funds in order to maintain their relationship with the hedge funds. In this regard, the court acknowledged that these derivative transactions could result in a hedge fund's ability to influence the vote of shares even when the funds had no direct ownership interests in those shares. Hence the court reasoned that such voting influence should be reported pursuant to Section 13(d).

The second issue in the case related to the extent to which the two hedge funds were acting as a group. Section 13(d) requires shareholders who act in concert for the purpose of holding or disposing of shares to make a disclosure as a group. Based on the timing of their purchases and meetings between the two funds, the court concluded that they had formed a group even though they did not have a formal agreement to act together, and thus were required to file appropriate disclosure.

While the case was heavily dependent on the particular facts, it demonstrates the court's willingness to both recognize and place limits on hedge funds' use of tactics that may involve empty voting or otherwise give such funds the ability to exert influence over transactions where they do not have a specific voting right connected to a company's stock. Moreover, the case reflects courts' concern about hedge funds' engagement in shareholder activism. The case opens with this statement: "Some people deliberately go close to the line dividing legal from illegal if they see sufficient opportunity for profit in doing so. A few cross that line, and if caught, seek to justify their actions on the basis of formalistic arguments even when it is apparent that they have defeated the purpose of the law. This is such a case. The defendants—to hedge funds that seek extraordinary gain, sometimes through 'shareholder activism'—amassed a large economic position ... for the purpose of causing CSX to behave in a manner that they hoped would lead to a rise in the value of their holdings."

To be sure, some insist that the criticisms levied against hedge funds are unwarranted, especially because hedge funds often act with the support of other investors. Yet hedge funds' success, coupled with their potential conflicts and use of risky tactics, has made their activism especially controversial.

The financial crisis has had an impact on hedge funds. Some claim that hedge funds played a significant role in that crisis, either causing or exacerbating it. Based on this claim, some have called for increased regulation of hedge funds, which could have an impact on their ability to engage in the type of aggressive activism in which they have historically engaged. To date, most of the regulatory changes do not significantly impact hedge funds' ability to continue their activist strategies. Even without that regulation, however, the financial crisis has diminished hedge funds' ability to engage in activism because that crisis has had an impact on hedge funds' financial health pursuant to which some funds have lost vast sums of money. Despite these and other potential changes, hedge funds have been key players in the recent surge in shareholder activism.

E. Activist Individuals

In addition to institutions, many individuals have played a prominent role as activist investors. Such activists often engage in campaigns through their leadership positions in hedge funds or other institutions. The following represents some individual shareholders who have had an impact on corporate governance:

Investor	Key Characteristics/Campaigns
William Ackman	Owner of hedge fund Pershing Square; waged Target proxy contest
Richard Breedan	Former SEC Chair; guided effort to broaden scope of shareholder resolutions relating to compensation and governance; waged AppleBee proxy contest
Warren Buffet	Primary shareholder and CEO of Berkshire Hathaway; emphasizes Value Investing for Shareholders; regarded as one of the most successful investors in the world
Sister Patricia Daly	Dominican Nun actively involved in Shareholder Proposal Campaigns to promote issues of corporate and social responsibility; negotiated with Exxon Mobil regarding human rights violations
Christopher Hohn	Managing partner of hedge fund Children's Investment Fund, known for donating a portion of its profits fee to charity; credited for forcing resignation of the CEO of German stock exchange Deutsche Borse; waged CSX proxy fight; involved in CSX lawsuit regarding impact of equity derivatives on beneficial ownership and impact of concerted investor activism on formation of group for disclosure purposes
Carl Icahn	Takeover artist turned shareholder activist; waged Yahoo proxy contest; created website The Icahn Report aimed at promoting shareholder activism; created United Shareholders of America, where individual investors can join campaign to enhance corporate governance
Daniel Loeb	Founder and manager of hedge fund Third Point LLC; known for letter writing campaign targeting company executives at underperforming companies
Nelson Peltz	Chairman of hedge fund Trian Group; former owner of Snapple; waged Heinz proxy contest
T. Boone Pickens	Takeover artist turned shareholder activist; head of hedge fund BP Capital Management; strong advocate of alternative energy; founded United Shareholders Association aimed at addressing important shareholder concerns

III. Proxy Advisory Firms

Proxy advisory firms are entities that assist shareholders in their voting decisions.[39] Such firms provide a range of services to shareholders, including making vote recommendations, developing voting guidelines for shareholders, researching corporate governance or other issues of shareholder concern, assisting with administrative aspects of voting and tracking shareholders' voting records, and coordinating the voting efforts of various institutional shareholders. Some shareholders also authorize proxy advisory firms to vote their proxy cards. Proxy advisory firms provide these services on a subscription fee basis.

Some proxy advisory firms also interact with corporations. In particular, such firms assist corporations with developing their corporate governance procedures. Some proxy advisory firms also rate companies' governance policies, and then provide services to help companies improve their ratings.

Although proxy advisory firms have been in existence since 1985, regulatory and market forces have dramatically increased the demand for such firms. In particular, in 2003 the SEC issued regulations requiring mutual funds to develop voting procedures, and to disclose their voting records on an annual basis.[40] Such regulations increased the need for proxy advisory services. In addition, institutional investors tend to rely heavily on proxy advisors for guidance because such advisors are perceived as having the resources and expertise necessary to analyze voting decisions at the wide variety of companies in which institutions hold shares. Thus, increases in institutional ownership have a corresponding increase in the role and influence of proxy advisory services.

RiskMetrics Group ("RiskMetrics"), founded in 1985 and formerly Institutional Shareholder Services ("ISS"), is the largest and most influential proxy advisory firm. One study indicates that in 2009, RiskMetrics issued proxy and vote recommendations for more than 37,000 shareholder meetings.[41] RiskMetrics also provides advice to more than 2,000 corporations.

Other proxy advisory firms include Glass Lewis & Co., which was founded in 2003 and is likely the largest competitor to RiskMetrics, and Proxy Governance, Inc. Both firms offer services to investors, but do not offer services to companies.

There has been growing concern regarding the influence of proxy advisory firms. Studies suggest that RiskMetrics and other proxy advisory firms have tremendous influence over shareholder voting, with some suggesting that these entities influence more than 30% of the shareholder vote. This kind of influence raises concerns because proxy advisory firms do not own any shares, do not vote, and thus are not accountable to shareholders or regulators. In particular, RiskMetrics has been criticized for the potential conflicts of interest involved with its provision of services to both shareholders and corporations.[42] Concerns also have been raised about the lack of transparency in the voting recommendations of proxy advisory firms.

Empirical evidence suggests that proxy advisory recommendations appear to be based on factors that should matter to investors.[43] However, that evidence also reveals that there is significant variation among the factors firms consider when making recommendations, and hence researchers warned that when shareholders choose proxy advisory firms, they should be aware of the many different variables advisors consider.[44]

At least one study also suggests that the power and influence of proxy advisors may have been overstated. Thus, it has been claimed that RiskMetrics influences as much as 30% of shareholder votes.[45] However, other researchers have found that while RiskMetrics appears to have the ability to influence 20% to 30% of the shareholder vote, this influence drops to 6% to 10% once other factors are taken into consideration.[46] To be sure, even these smaller percentages suggest that proxy advisory firms play an important role in shareholder voting.

CHAPTER 5

SHAREHOLDER PROPOSALS: A PLATFORM FOR COMMUNICATION AND CHANGE

Shareholder proposals are recommendations related to corporate policies that appear on the corporate proxy statement to be voted on by shareholders. Such proposals are critical to the shareholder empowerment movement. Because most shareholders at public companies attend the annual meeting by proxy, the annual meeting does not serve as a forum through which shareholders can communicate their views to the corporation. Instead, the proxy statement serves at that forum. Shareholder proposals appear on the proxy statement. Thus, shareholder proposals represent the primary means by which shareholders express their views regarding important corporate issues and propose changes to corporate policy. Moreover, because corporations pay for the cost of distributing the proxy statement, the shareholder proposal process is subsidized by the corporation, and thus almost every shareholder can take advantage of the shareholder proposal process. In fact, virtually every major shareholder initiative has been advanced through the shareholder proposal arena.

Shareholder proposals serve at least three purposes. First, they highlight shareholder views on important issues impacting the corporation. In this regard, both the nature of the proposals and the relative shareholder support for those proposals reflect important information for corporations. Second, shareholder proposals enhance communication among shareholders and between the corporation and shareholders. As this section demonstrates, most shareholder proposals are advisory in nature. Thus, corporations are not required to implement such proposals even when they receive majority shareholder support. Shareholder proposals nevertheless are critical because they may prompt dialogue between shareholders and the corporation about critical issues, thereby increasing shareholders' role in corporate affairs. Third, shareholder proposals can influence corporate policy. Indeed, shareholders hope that by communicating and generating significant shareholder support for their views, they will prompt corporations to make changes to corporate policy. In recent years, shareholders have managed to successfully use the proposal process to encourage corporations to alter a range of corporate policies. Shareholders' reliance on the proposal process therefore has significantly altered the corporate governance landscape in ways that have increased shareholders' voting power and authority within the corporation.

The first portion of this chapter discusses the shareholder proposal rule from its historical roots to its modern format and application. The second portion examines the manner in which shareholders have utilized the shareholder proposal rule to increase their voice within the corporation. The third section highlights some of the key issues that have been advanced through the proposal process.

I. The Shareholder Proposal Rule

The federal proxy rules enable shareholders to submit proposals that will appear on the corporation's proxy statement and be voted on during a shareholder meeting. The shareholder proposal rule can be found under Rule 14a-8 of the Exchange Act ("Rule 14a-8"). Rule 14a-8 defines a shareholder proposal as shareholders' recommendation or requirement that a company and/or its directors take certain action.[1] Because most corporate statutes give shareholders the ability to amend the corporation's bylaws, many shareholder proposals involve changes to the bylaws. The term "proposal" includes both the requested change and any statements shareholders make in support of that change.

The shareholder proposal rule has evolved over time. The SEC first adopted federal rules governing proxies in 1935, but those rules did not contain a shareholder proposal provision.[2] However, the SEC soon expressed concern about this omission. In the SEC's view, because the proxy statement "purports to tell the stockholders everything that is going to be taken up at the meeting," it would be "obviously misleading" to exclude from the proxy statement shareholder proposals about which the corporation was aware.[3] This view prompted the SEC to adopt a rule requiring disclosure of shareholder proposals in 1942.[4] Since that time, the shareholder proposal rule has undergone several changes. In terms of the rule's format, two changes are particularly noteworthy. In 1976, the SEC revised the shareholder proposal rule to identify several rationales on which corporations could rely to exclude shareholder proposals from the proxy statement.[5] In 1998, the SEC reorganized the rule into a question and answer format designed to make it more understandable.[6] Consistent with these changes, the current version of Rule 14a-8 appears in a question and answer format and contains procedural and substantive bases for exclusion of shareholder proposals. This section discusses those bases.

A. Procedural Rules

Rule 14a-8 contains several procedural hurdles that shareholders must clear in order to make use of the shareholder proposal rule. First, by the date of submission, shareholders must hold at least $2000 in market value or 1%t of the company's securities entitled to vote on the proposal, and must have done so continuously for at least one year.[7] This holding requirement was enacted in 1983 to ensure that only shareholders with long-term interest in the corporation be allowed to use the shareholder proposal rule.[8] Second, each eligible shareholder may only submit one proposal per shareholders' meeting.[9] This rule also was adopted in 1983 to prevent shareholders from cluttering the corporate proxy statement.

Third, a shareholder proposal can be no more than five hundred words.[10] The word limit is aimed at controlling the expense associated with including shareholder proposals on a company's proxy statement. Shareholders use the five hundred word limit to include supporting statements aimed at encouraging other shareholders to support their proposals. The word limit includes titles or headings to the proposal if they can be construed as arguments in support of the proposal. Shareholders also can reference a website in their proposal so long as the site and any references within the site do not contain materially false or misleading information. A website generally counts as one word. The corporation can and often does include on the proxy statement its response to the shareholder's proposal as well as its recommendation regarding how shareholders should vote on the proposal. While Rule 14a-8 does not impose a word limit on the corporation's response, shareholders' response to the corporation must be incorporated into the five hundred word limit.

Shareholders also must comply with the proposal deadline. Generally, if the proposal is to be submitted in connection with an annual meeting, the proposal must be submitted not less than 120 calendar days before the date of the prior year's proxy statement.[11] This deadline usually can be found in last year's proxy statement.

In addition, either the shareholder who submitted the proposal, or a representative, must personally appear at the shareholders' meeting to present the proposal.[12] If the corporation holds any portion of its meeting electronically and permits the proposal to be presented electronically, then the shareholder also can appear via electronic media. If a shareholder fails to appear in person without good cause, a corporation can exclude any proposals she submits for the next two calendar years.

B. Substantive Rules

Interestingly, the initial shareholder proposal rule did not include any limitation on the type of proposals shareholders could submit. However, the rule slowly evolved to include various substantive reasons why a corporation could exclude a shareholder proposal. Rule 14a-8 currently contains thirteen substantive exclusions as identified in Part II.

C. Process Associated with Excluding Proposals

As a general matter there is a presumption in favor of allowing shareholders to submit proposals to the corporate proxy statement. Thus, if a corporation wants to exclude a proposal, the burden is on the corporation to demonstrate that the exclusion is appropriate.

The process for exclusions based on procedural defects is slightly different than that associated with substantive problems. If a corporation wishes to exclude a shareholder proposal based on the shareholder's failure to meet procedural requirements, the corporation must notify the shareholder of the procedural defect within fourteen days of receiving the proposal, and give the shareholder at least fourteen days to correct or cure the defect.[13] However, if a defect cannot be cured—such as if a shareholder fails to submit a proposal within the deadline—the corporation need not provide any notice to the shareholder.

Once a corporation has made the decision to exclude a proposal, the corporation must simultaneously notify both the SEC and the submitting shareholder. With respect to procedural defects, corporations make this notification after they have complied with the requirements for giving shareholders an opportunity to cure as indicated above. If a corporation wants to exclude a proposal for a substantive reason, there is no process for curing the proposal. Thus, the corporation begins the exclusion process with the notice to the SEC. The corporation's notice to the SEC must be made no later than 80 calendar days before it files its definitive proxy statement. The notice must include the reasons for exclusion as well as supporting legal opinions if such reasons are based on state or foreign law. Shareholders are permitted, but not required, to make their own submission to the SEC responding to the corporation's arguments.

When the corporation submits its reasons for excluding the proposal, it can make a no-action request. The no-action request letter is submitted to the SEC's Division of Corporate Finance staff. The SEC staff does not have to respond to a no-action request. If the SEC staff does respond, it will either agree with the company's assertions or indicate that it cannot concur in the company's assessment. The staff's agreement means that, based on the circumstances identified by the corporation, the staff concludes that it will not recommend that the SEC take enforcement action against the corporation for a failure to include a given proposal. Essentially a favorable no-action letter gives a corporation comfort that it can exclude a shareholder proposal without repercussions. The SEC staff will not issue such a letter when there is pending litigation, or when the law is unsettled on a particular matter. If the SEC staff refuses to issue a no-action letter or indicates that it does not concur with the corporation, then the corporation must make a decision to exclude the proposal despite that refusal. If the SEC staff responds in this manner, most corporations will include a shareholder proposal. Because they reflect the views of the SEC staff as opposed to the SEC, no-action letters are non-binding. However, the SEC staff reviews prior no-action letters involving similar issues and often follows recommendations made in such letters. Thus, corporations and shareholders often submit other no-action letters along with their no-action request. The SEC makes no-action letters available to the public.[14] Either the company or the shareholder can seek review of the SEC's no-action decision in a federal district court.

II. Notable Substantive Exclusions

As the following chart reveals, there are thirteen substantive reasons on which corporations can rely to exclude a proposal.

Rule 14a-8(i) If I have complied with the procedural requirements, on what other bases may a company rely to exclude my proposal?
(1) **Improper under state law:** If the proposal is not a proper subject for action by shareholders under the laws of the jurisdiction of the company's organization;
(2) **Violation of law:** If the proposal would, if implemented, cause the company to violate any state, federal, or foreign law to which it is subject;

(3) **Violation of proxy rules:** If the proposal or supporting statement is contrary to any of the Commission's proxy rules, including § 240.14a-9, which prohibits materially false or misleading statements in proxy soliciting materials;

(4) **Personal grievance; special interest:** If the proposal relates to the redress of a personal claim or grievance against the company or any other person, or if it is designed to result in a benefit to you, or to further a personal interest, which is not shared by the other shareholders at large;

(5) **Relevance:** If the proposal relates to operations which account for less than 5 percent of the company's total assets at the end of its most recent fiscal year, and for less than 5 percent of its net earnings and gross sales for its most recent fiscal year, and is not otherwise significantly related to the company's business;

(6) **Absence of power/authority:** If the company would lack the power or authority to implement the proposal;

(7) **Management functions:** If the proposal deals with a matter relating to the company's ordinary business operations;

(8) **Relates to election:** If the proposal relates to a nomination or an election for membership on the company's board of directors or analogous governing body or a procedure for such nomination or election;**As in effect on 8/24/2010

(9) **Conflicts with company's proposal:** If the proposal directly conflicts with one of the company's own proposals to be submitted to shareholders at the same meeting;

(10) **Substantially implemented:** If the company has already substantially implemented the proposal;

(11) **Duplication:** If the proposal substantially duplicates another proposal previously submitted to the company by another proponent that will be included in the company's proxy materials for the same meeting;

(12) **Resubmissions:** If the proposal deals with substantially the same subject matter as another proposal or proposals that has or have been previously included in the company's proxy materials within the preceding 5 calendar years, a company may exclude it from its proxy materials for any meeting held within 3 calendar years of the last time it was included if the proposal received:

(i) Less than 3% of the vote if proposed once within the preceding 5 calendar years;

(ii) Less than 6% of the vote on its last submission to shareholders if proposed twice previously within the preceding 5 calendar years; or

(iii) Less than 10% of the vote on its last submission to shareholders if proposed three times or more previously within the preceding 5 calendar years; and

(13) **Specific amount of dividends:** If the proposal relates to specific amounts of cash or stock dividends.

Corporations often pinpoint more than one reason when seeking to justify exclusion. This section highlights some of the substantive rules that have been particularly significant throughout the years.

A. Conflicts with State or Other Laws

Five years after the SEC implemented the shareholder proposal rule, it amended the rule to impose the first limitation on the type of proposals that shareholders could include on the proxy statement. That limitation is codified in Rule 14a-8(i)(1) and allows corporations to exclude proposals if they are not a proper subject for shareholder action under state law.

This exclusion explains why the vast majority of shareholder proposals are advisory or precatory in nature, as opposed to binding. Under state law, directors have wide discretion to manage the corporation, and shareholders do not have the ability to direct corporate affairs or otherwise require directors and officers to take specific actions. In light of this state law limitation on shareholder authority, proposals mandating certain actions are considered excludable as improper subjects for shareholder action under state law. Thus, a shareholder proposal that would require corporations to amend the bylaws or take particular action would be viewed as improper under state law and hence excludable. By contrast, proposals that only recommend or request certain actions would be viewed as proper under Rule 14a-8(i)(1). Hence, as a result of this rule, shareholders generally craft their proposals in terms of recommendations as opposed to binding requirements.

Rule 14a-8(i)(2) also influences shareholders' decisions to refrain from submitting binding shareholder proposals. That Rule permits exclusion of proposals that, if implemented, would cause the corporation to violate state, federal, or foreign laws to which it was subject. If a shareholder proposal would cause directors to breach their fiduciary duty, it would be viewed as violating this rule. Given directors' broad discretion, courts have reasoned that some binding proposals prevent directors from exercising their own judgment, which in turn undermines their ability to exercise their fiduciary duty to act in the corporation's best interests. Consequently, such binding proposals would violate Rule 14a-8(i)(2). In order to avoid this result, shareholders structure their proposals regarding corporate actions as recommendations.

Rule 14a-8(i)(2) also operates to ensure that proposals are crafted so that they only apply to future action. Indeed, if a proposal would cause a corporation to breach a current contract, then it would be excludable under this section. This often means that shareholders must be careful to draft their proposals so that they only relate to future conduct.

Recently, shareholders have sought to introduce binding shareholder proposals covering particular corporate policies. There are some circumstances under which such proposals make it onto the corporate proxy statement. First, if a corporation does not seek to exclude the proposal, then it will be included. Second, even if a corporation challenges the validity of the proposal, if state law is unclear regarding whether the proposal is a proper subject for shareholder action or would violate state law, the SEC will refuse to issue a no-action letter or otherwise sanction exclusion of a proposal under Rule 14a-8(i)(1) or Rule 14a-8(i)(2). Because most corporations will not exclude proposals when the SEC staff refuses to issue a no-action letter, any lack of clarity surrounding these rules often has the effect of enabling shareholders to include such proposals, even when they are binding.

Delaware recently created a system aimed at facilitating the SEC's review of proposals impacting state law. In 2007, Delaware established a system permitting the SEC to certify questions of Delaware law directly to the Delaware Supreme Court.[15] The certification process facilitates the shareholder proposal process by enabling the SEC to gain a definitive answer on unsettled areas of Delaware law, and thus to make a ruling on the excludability of a proposal under the first two provisions of the shareholder proposal rule.

The SEC used this process for the first time in 2008. In that year, CA, Inc., a Delaware corporation ("CA"), sought to exclude a binding proposal from one of its shareholders that, if approved, would require CA to reimburse shareholders' expenses related to election campaigns as long as certain conditions were met. Harvard Professor Lucian Bebchuk helped draft the proposal, and was a key supporter of the proposal's validity under the proxy rules. However, CA's counsel insisted that the rule violated state law.

In light of these conflicting interpretations of Delaware law, the SEC certified the following two questions to the Delaware Supreme Court: (1) whether a binding resolution related to reimbursement of shareholder expenses incurred in an election campaign was a proper subject for action under Delaware law, and (2) if implemented, whether the binding provision would cause the corporation to violate Delaware law.[16] The Delaware Supreme Court concluded that the bylaw was a proper subject for shareholder action because shareholders have a legitimate interest in bylaws that serve to facilitate their participation in board elections. Such a conclusion meant that the shareholder proposal did not violate Rule 14a-8(i)(1). However, the Delaware Supreme Court also concluded that the bylaw amendment as proposed would cause the corporation to violate state law because it would limit the board's discretion.[17] Hence, the shareholder proposal would violate Rule 14a-8(i)(2). After the decision, the SEC issued a letter indicating that it would take no action if CA excluded the proposal. This decision demonstrates the interplay between the first two shareholder proposal exclusions. It also demonstrates the manner in which Delaware has facilitated review of the shareholder proposal process.

B. The Ordinary Business Exclusion

The so-called ordinary business exclusion, encompassed in Rule 14a-8(i)(7), represents one of the most heavily litigated and debated shareholder proposal exclusions. The Rule allows corporations to exclude proposals if they deal with matters relating to the company's "ordinary business operations." Most shareholder proposals get excluded as a result of the ordinary business rule. The SEC first adopted the rule in 1954 in order to ensure that shareholder proposals did not cover matters that should be left to the discretion of management. However, the SEC often struggles with determining the dividing line between matters that encompass ordinary business operations and those that do not. This struggle has been particularly pronounced in two areas: social/political matters and employment matters.

Initially, the SEC took the position that all shareholder proposals addressing social or political matters should be viewed as falling within the board's ordinary business operations and thus should be excludable. However, the SEC soon altered its position, reasoning that some issues were so significant that they should not fall within the range of ordinary business matters. Hence, when public debate makes a social or political issue significant, proposals related to that issue will not be excludable. This interpretation has allowed a broad range of social issues to appear on the proxy statement in the context of shareholder proposals. The interpretation also means that whether an issue is excludable evolves as public opinion on that issue evolves.

The ordinary business exclusion also has impacted employment matters. The SEC initially took the position that day to day employment matters were excludable as ordinary business decisions unless they related to significant social policies. Compensation matters involving executives would be deemed to fall outside of the exclusion because of the clear concern about executive compensation. However, compensation arrangements relating to rank and file employees likely would fall within the exclusion unless they involved some clear social policy. This approach led to a case by case assessment of shareholder proposals impacting employment issues.

And then came the case of Cracker Barrel. In 1991, Cracker Barrel announced that it would no longer employ individuals "whose sexual preferences fail to demonstrate normal heterosexual values," and then fired several employees based on their sexual orientation. Eventually shareholders submitted a proposal to be included on Cracker Barrel's proxy statement, requesting that Cracker Barrel adopt an antidiscrimination policy covering sexual orientation. Cracker Barrel sought to exclude the proposal. In 1992, the SEC staff issued a no-action letter supporting Cracker Barrel's decision, noting that it fell under the ordinary business exclusion because it related to everyday employment matters. The letter reflected an abrupt change in its approach of allowing employment proposals that were tied to social issues to be removed from the ordinary business exclusion. However, the SEC staff contended that such an approach had been unworkable and had essentially nullified the application of the ordinary business rule because it had allowed almost all employment-related proposals to be included on the proxy statement under the guise that they involved some social policy. As a result, in its Cracker Barrel no-action letter the SEC announced the adoption of a bright-line test pursuant to which proposals related to everyday employment matters would be excludable, while those involving executives would be allowed.

The decision was so controversial that eventually the SEC reversed itself again. Thus, in 1998, the SEC abandoned its bright-line test for a more case by case analysis of employment-related shareholder proposals. As with proposals involving social issues, the SEC clearly acknowledges that this case by case approach means that whether an employment-related shareholder proposal is excludable depends on whether public debate has made the issues addressed by the proposal significant.[18]

C. Relevance

Another prominent rule has been Rule 14a-8(i)(7), which is aimed at ensuring that only issues relevant to the corporation and its operations appear on the proxy statement. The original version of this rule was aimed specifically at excluding social proposals. In 1951, shareholders of Greyhound sought to include a proposal requesting that the Greyhound bus company abolish segregation on its buses. The SEC issued a no-action letter permitting Greyhound to exclude the proposal. The issues involved with the exclusion prompted the SEC to adopt a rule in 1952 permitting the exclusion of proposals aimed at promoting "economic, political, racial, religious or social causes."

Eventually, however, the SEC recognized that there were some social issues that were relevant to the corporation and its operation, and hence shifted its stance with respect to exclusion of proposals involving these issues. First, the SEC completely abandoned the 1952 rule. In its place, the SEC adopted a rule permitting the exclusion of proposals based on an objective relevance test. Second, in 1982, the SEC amended the rule adding language to make clear that even when proposals fail to meet the objective relevance test, they could not be excluded if they related to matters which were "otherwise significant." Thus, the current version of Rule 14a-8(i)(7) provides that a proposal can be excluded if it "relates to operations which account for less than 5 percent of the company's total assets at the end of its most recent fiscal year, and for less than 5 percent of its net earnings and gross sales for its most recent fiscal year, and is not otherwise significantly related to the company's business." The SEC stated that the inclusion of the "otherwise significant" language was aimed at preventing the automatic exclusion of proposals relating to socially significant matters. The amended language has had the effect of allowing shareholders to submit social proposals across a broad range of issues. This includes proposals pertaining to the force-feeding of geese, the use of napalm, and operations in regions engaging in human rights or other violations.

D. Elections

Rule 14a-8(i)(8) enables corporations to exclude from the proxy statement shareholder proposals relating to director elections. According to the SEC, the purpose of the exclusion is to prevent shareholders from using the shareholder proposal apparatus to wage election contests. As a result of the rule, shareholders cannot use the shareholder proposal rules to nominate candidates of their choice to the corporation's proxy statement.

This election exclusion has been the subject of considerable controversy and shareholder activism. Because of the rule, if a shareholder would like to nominate a candidate who is not supported by management, the shareholder must prepare and distribute her own proxy statement, and wage a proxy contest. Empirical evidence suggests that financial costs and other barriers prohibit all but a few shareholders from engaging in a proxy contest. Because the election exclusion effectively limits shareholders to nominating directors through a proxy contest, shareholders contend that the exclusion undermines their ability to influence elections. Shareholders have argued that their lack of access to the proxy statement means that most directors are nominated by management and run unopposed. In this regard, shareholders view the election exclusion as one that ensures that shareholders simply rubber stamp the choices of management. Hence, shareholders have repeatedly sought to alter the rule to enable them to gain access to the corporation's proxy statement.

The SEC's stance on this issue has shifted throughout the years. One important question left open by the rule is the extent to which it enables shareholders to include proposals that seek to establish *procedures* for establishing access to the proxy statement. When the shareholder proposal rule was originally adopted, the SEC took the position that such proposals did not run afoul of the election exclusion. However, in 1976, the SEC staff began excluding such proposals on the basis that they would create future election contests and thereby violated the proposal rules.

In response to increased shareholder pressure to alter the rule, in 2007 the SEC invited comments on two conflicting rule changes related to Rule 14a-8(i)(8).[19] One proposal would have amended Rule 14a-8 to permit inclusion of shareholder proposals in the company's proxy materials relating to bylaws mandating procedures for shareholders to nominate candidates to the board.[20] The second proposal would have amended Rule 14a-8 to make clear that corporations could exclude from their proxy statement any proposal for a bylaw aimed at adopting procedures for allowing shareholder access to the ballot.[21] The SEC ultimately embraced the second proposal.

In 2010, in connection with other reforms facilitating director elections, the SEC amended the rule again in order to enable shareholders to submit proposals addressing procedures for shareholders to nominate directors on the proxy statement, essentially reversing the position it had endorsed three years prior. Unlike the 2007 proposed rule, however, the 2010 rule completely altered the content of Rule 14a-8(i)(8). The SEC has issued a stay on the rules implementation because various groups have challenged the validity of the rule. The chart below reflects the recent evolution of Rule 14a-8(i)(8).

Comparison of Changes to Rule 14a8(i)(8)

In effect as of June 2007	As amended on November 28, 2007	As amended on August 25, 2010
(8) Director elections: If the proposal relates to an election for membership on the company's board of directors or analogous governing body;	**(8) Director elections:** If the proposal relates to a nomination or an election for membership on the company's board of directors or analogous governing body or a procedure for such nomination or election;	**(8) Director elections:** If the proposal: (i) Would disqualify a nominee who is standing for election; (ii) Would remove a director from office before his or her term expired; (iii) Questions the competence, business judgment, or character of one or more nominees or directors; (iv) Seeks to include a specific individual in the company's proxy materials for election to the board of directors; or (v) Otherwise could affect the outcome of the upcoming election of directors.

III. Evolution of the Shareholder Proposal Rule

Historically, the shareholder proposal apparatus was used primarily by shareholders seeking to raise concerns about social or political issues. For example, shareholders used the proposal process in the

1950s to raise concerns about racial discrimination and segregation. Later, shareholders used the proposal process to pressure corporations to divest from South Africa and to raise awareness of apartheid. Shareholder efforts to focus attention on these causes at times translated into success. Indeed, perhaps the most successful campaign in this area was the one seeking to encourage corporations to divest from South Africa. Shareholder proposals requesting reports on corporate activity in South Africa and its impact on the community increasingly gained support, ranging from 25% to near 70% in the 1990s. Many attribute that kind of support to one of the key reasons why corporations began divesting from South Africa.

More recently, governance-oriented proposals have dominated the shareholder proposal landscape. Some attribute this domination to the rise of institutional investors, while others attribute this domination to recent governance scandals and the perceived need to hold corporate officers and directors more accountable. This section highlights some of the key governance proposals advocated by shareholders.

A. Say on Pay and Other Compensation-Related Proposals

In the past few years, compensation proposals have dominated the proposal landscape. Thus, since 2004, executive compensation has been the number one issue addressed by shareholder proposals. In 2009, shareholders filed more than two hundred pay-related proposals.[22]

The compensation-related proposals receiving the most attention, however, has been say on pay—those related to an advisory vote on executive compensation. Over the last three proxy seasons, there were a record number of say on pay proposals. In 2010, say on pay proposals were the most prevalent type of compensation proposal as well as the most dominate type of shareholder proposal submitted. Shareholder support for say on pay proposals went from 42% in 2008 to 46% in 2009.[23]

Many companies have voluntarily adopted say on pay provisions. In 2008, only six companies had voluntarily adopted say on pay. Aflac was the first company to voluntarily adopt say on pay as well as the first to hold a say on pay vote. By the end of 2010, more than fifty companies had voluntarily adopted say on pay, although some companies have opted to hold votes either every two years, or in the case of Microsoft, every three years.

The support behind say on pay prompted the federal government to mandate say on pay. In 2009, companies receiving funding under TARP were required to provide their shareholders with an annual say on pay vote throughout the period during which such companies receive funds.[24] This meant that some four hundred companies were required to provide a say on pay vote. The July 2010 Dodd-Frank Act mandated say on pay for all public companies.[25] Under the Dodd-Frank Act, public companies must provide shareholders with a say on pay vote at least once every three years, and must provide shareholders with a non-binding vote on whether the company should hold a say on pay vote every one, two, or three years.[26]

Shareholders have pressed for say on pay because they believe it will curtail the rise in executive compensation, while encouraging corporations to more closely link executive pay with corporate performance. Indeed, recent years have generated significant public outrage with what has been perceived as excessive executive compensation. Say on pay has been one key response to this outrage. In the UK where say on pay has been mandated since 2002, evidence suggests that such votes have more closely connected pay with performance.[27] Many question whether similar results can be expected in the US. Moreover, others argue that the UK experience has revealed problematic practices, such as the failure of say on pay to more closely align pay and compensation rates at well-performing companies, as well as an over-reliance on compensation consultants and best practices that could produce inefficient pay practices.[28] Nevertheless, the apparent success of the UK experience has spurred support for say on pay.

Despite controversy surrounding executive pay packages, until very recently most shareholders overwhelmingly approved pay packages. In 2009, not a single public company lost a say on pay vote, despite considerable discontent surrounding executive pay. Moreover, most shareholders approved pay packages with 90% or more of the shareholder vote. However, in 2010, shareholders for the first time rejected pay packages at three companies: Occidental Petroleum, KeyCorp, and Motorola. As of February 2011, shareholders also had rejected pay packages at Jacobs Engineering Group and Beazer Homes USA.

As data calculated by RiskMetrics Group indicates, other compensation-related proposals include the following:[29]

- Banking of executive bonuses that would defer executive bonuses for several years (25% shareholder support in 2009)
- Pay for performance proposals (24% shareholder support in 2008)
- Minimum holding/retention period (beyond retirement) for stock awards (26% shareholder support in 2009)
- Establish an anti-gross up policy (53% shareholder support in 2009)
- Shareholder approval of golden parachutes (36% shareholder support in 2009, down from 50% in 2008)
- Shareholder approval of executive death benefits—so-called "golden coffin" (38% shareholder support in 2009)
- Claw-back provisions that recoup executive bonuses after financial restatements (10% shareholder support in 2008)
- Removal of CEO from compensation committee

B. Majority Voting

As Chapter 6 reveals in further detail, shareholders used the proposal process to encourage corporations to implement majority voting.

C. Classified Boards

Since the hostile takeover battles, shareholders have been pushing to eliminate classified or staggered boards—boards in which shareholders only elect a percentage of the directors each year. Shareholders view classified boards as a form of managerial entrenchment because such a structure makes it difficult to oust the entire board in a single year. Thus, shareholders have been submitting proposals on this issue since the 1980s. Since 2000, such proposals have consistently garnered more than 50% shareholder support, with an average shareholder support of 63% in 2009.[30] While historical studies revealed that many corporations retained their classified boards despite shareholder support for declassification,[31] more recent studies reveal that annual elections are becoming more prevalent. Hence, while most S&P 500 companies had classified boards in 2000, by the end of 2006, shareholders elected a majority of directors at S&P 500 companies annually.

D. Other Governance Proposals

1. Special Meetings: Many companies either only allow directors to call special meetings or provide that such meetings may only be called by shareholders holding 25% or more of the company's stock. Shareholders have requested the right to call special meetings so long as they hold a specified percentage of stock, generally 10%. Shareholders believe that this right is critical because it ensures that they can vote on key issues, such as the election or removal of directors, during periods outside of the annual meeting. Proposals on this issue averaged 50% shareholder support in 2009.[32]

2. Eliminate Supermajority Vote Requirements: Many corporate documents require that certain transactions be approved only by a "supermajority of the shareholder vote"—a vote in excess of a majority such as 60% or 75%. Shareholders have sought the elimination of these requirements so that they can more easily influence such transactions. Proposals on this issue averaged 69% shareholder support in 2009.[33]

3. Independent Board Chair: Shareholders have sought to require that corporations separate the position of board chair and CEO based on concerns that combining the position increases the likelihood that the board is dominated by the CEO, and hence may not feel free to exercise independent judgment. Proposals on this issue averaged 36% shareholder support in 2009.[34]

4. Succession Planning: Shareholders also have been pressuring boards to disclose their succession plans for CEOs and other top executives.

5. Reincorporation in North Dakota: Although it has not garnered significant shareholder support, some shareholders have sought to re-incorporate in North Dakota because that state passed a shareholder-friendly corporate code that includes provisions allowing for proxy access and other rights advocated by shareholders. Proposals on this issue averaged 7% shareholder support in 2009.[35]

E. The Persistence of Social Proposals

While governance proposals have come to dominate the proposal process in recent years, there still remains vibrant activity for proposals regarding social and political issues. Indeed, there have been an increasing number of social proposals, coupled with increased shareholder support for such proposals.[36] Importantly, social proposals rarely received high levels of support, and most never received support in excess of 20%. However, recently the average support for social proposals has neared 30%, while several shareholder proposals have achieved record levels of support.

Importantly, the "success" of social proposals often is not measured by its ability to garner majority support. Instead, if such proposals manage to obtain 20% or 30% shareholder support, such support may be sufficient to prompt corporations to dialogue with shareholders about a particular social proposal. Moreover, success is also measured by the number of withdrawn proposals. A withdrawn proposal often indicates that corporations and shareholders have reached an agreement on the proposal issue, or otherwise that the corporation has indicated its willingness to address shareholder concerns related to that issue. In this respect, withdrawals are often a positive development. Recent years have involved record levels of withdrawn social proposals.

The following reflects a representative sample of some of the key social issues that have garnered attention in recent years.

1. Climate Change: In 2009, a climate change proposal received majority support for the first time.[37] In 2008, such a proposal

achieved a record 45% of the shareholder vote. Climate change proposals generally involve a request that the corporation create plans or set goals for the reduction of greenhouse gas emissions.

2. Sustainability: Proposals associated with sustainability issues received an average support of 19% in 2009.[38]

3. Political Contributions: In light of the Supreme Court's 2010 decision in *Citizens United v. Federal Election Commission*, holding that the federal government cannot prohibit corporate spending in political campaigns, there has been a surge of proposals related to political spending, and disclosure about corporate contributions and policies surrounding contributions. Such proposals averaged 29% shareholder support in 2009, with three proposals receiving as much as 39% shareholder support.[39]

4. Board Diversity: Shareholders routinely submit proposals seeking information on board diversity, and on corporate policies and procedures associated with diversity.

5. Nondiscrimination Policies: Shareholders also submit proposals seeking information on nondiscrimination policies, including policies focused on sexual orientation. In 2009, proposals asking companies to outlaw discrimination based on sexual orientation and gender identity accounted for the most number of withdrawn proposals.[40]

IV. The Impact of Shareholder Proposals

On the one hand, shareholders have managed to use the shareholder proposal process to generate significant changes in the corporation and its governance structure. This suggests that such proposals have tremendous impact.

On the other hand, most of the empirical evidence reveals that shareholder proposals have little impact on a company's financial performance, either in the short term or in the long term. Some studies indicate some positive short-term stock price reaction, depending on the subject matter of the proposal. Yet most others find no significant stock price reaction to shareholder proposals, while others have found a negative reaction.[41]

Similarly, many studies reveal no long-term impact on a company's operating, stock or accounting performance as a result of being the target of shareholder proposal activity.[42] Other studies that reveal positive long-term results have been criticized for their methodology. To be sure, it is too soon to tell how the most recent corporate changes will impact corporate performance. Nevertheless, this data raises important questions about the benefits of shareholder proposals.

V. Future Outlook for the Shareholder Proposal Rule

Some have advocated abolishing the shareholder proposal rule because it can be a costly distraction, enabling shareholders to submit nuisance proposals or otherwise generate discontent around issues of questionable significance to the corporation and its bottom line. Such advocacy may be legitimized by empirical studies indicating that such proposals may have no considerable impact on corporate performance.

However, the proposal rules appear to play a critical role in shareholder communications, representing an important platform for shareholders to express their views and advocate for particular issues. The rule also has enabled shareholders to make corporate governance changes they deemed to be important. Thus, it is unlikely that the rule will be abolished or even sharply curtailed. Instead, shareholders will continue to rely on the rule to enhance their voice within the corporate lexicon.

CHAPTER 6

THE MAJORITY VOTE MOVEMENT

I. Plurality Voting

Under most corporate statutes, the default rule is that share-holders elect directors under a plurality system. The plurality system means that directors are elected so long as they receive a plurality of the votes cast, without regard to votes withheld or cast against them. Thus, in an uncontested election, plurality voting ensures that a director will be elected so long as she receives *any* votes in her favor, even if ninety percent or more of the shareholders vote against her.

Plurality voting became the default standard primarily to prevent failed elections.[1] Given the dispersed nature of public shareholders, a rule requiring directors to receive a majority vote could result in no director receiving the requisite number of votes to be victorious, leaving a company without members to serve on its board. The possibility of a failed election is most relevant when there is an election contest because the existence of multiple candidates creates a greater potential that votes will be cast in such a way that no one director receives a majority. Hence, the plurality standard was deemed the most effective to ensure successful board elections.

Although plurality voting was the default rule, state corporate statutes allowed corporations to alter the rule by adopting a standard requiring that candidates receive more than a plurality of the votes in order to become a director. However, historically the vast majority of corporations chose to adhere to a plurality voting system.[2]

II. Vote No Campaigns

In "Vote No" or "Withhold the Vote" campaigns, shareholders are encouraged to withhold their votes against a particular director or particular directors. The federal proxy rules do not require corporations to provide a means for shareholders to vote against directors.[3] However, proxy rules do require that voting or "proxy" cards enable shareholders to withhold their votes from directors.[4] Vote no campaigns take advantage of this requirement, allowing shareholders to collectively target particular directors.

A 1992 SEC rule change bolstered the viability of vote no campaigns by creating broad exemptions for shareholder communications that do not involve actual proxy solicitations.[5] Such a rule change allows shareholders to communicate with one another regarding their voting preferences without being burdened with the costs associated with engaging in a proxy solicitation. The rule change therefore allows shareholders to actively encourage their fellow shareholders to withhold their votes against particular directors, thereby enhancing the potential success of vote no campaigns.

In recent years, shareholders have demonstrated an increased willingness to withhold their votes from directors. In 2009, shareholders withheld more than 10% of their votes from directors at 93 S&P 500 companies, an increase from 82 in 2008, 64 in 2007, and 57 in 2006.[6] Moreover, in 2009, shareholders withheld a majority of their support from 91 directors, almost three times the number of directors who failed to obtain majority support in 2008.[7] The 2009 numbers represented a record high number of directors failing to receive majority shareholder support.

Shareholders use vote no campaigns to convey their discontent with specific directors, particular decisions, or overall corporate policy. In this regard, such campaigns represent an important vehicle for communicating with the board and management. For example, the 2009 surge in vote withholding appears to reflect shareholders' efforts to convey their dissatisfaction regarding executive compensation.[8] Thus, shareholders withheld votes from directors at firms in which the compensation packages appeared problematic.

Of course, under a plurality voting system, a vote no campaign does not directly impact director elections because such a system enables directors to be elected without regard to dissenting votes. Hence, even if shareholders withhold a majority of their votes against directors, such withholding does not directly result in directors losing their board seats. At most, therefore, vote no campaigns that occur within a plurality system represent an indirect means of impacting boards.

However, proponents insist that vote no campaigns can have a significant impact on election outcomes and broader corporate policies. In his 1993 *Stanford Law Review* article, former SEC Commissioner and Law Professor Joseph Grundfest urged shareholders to take advantage of vote no campaigns.[9] He believed that such campaigns represented an ideal mechanism for expressing votes of no confidence in the existing management and board. As Professor Grundfest put it, "properly conducted, just vote no campaigns can thus become annual referenda on the quality of American management and transform the annual shareholder meeting from an empty ritual into a valuable medium for the exercise of shareholder voice."[10]

Importantly, Professor Grundfest insisted that such campaigns reflected an appropriate exercise of shareholder power precisely because they worked within the plurality voting structure. Indeed, Professor Grundfest believed that, by working within such structure, vote no campaigns struck the right balance between shareholder accountability and board autonomy. On the one hand, such campaigns give shareholders a relatively inexpensive means of impacting corporate affairs. Indeed, an important benefit of a vote no campaign is that shareholders need not garner a majority of withheld votes in order to have an impact. Instead, large percentages of withheld votes could be sufficient to signal shareholder discontent, prompting the board to communicate with shareholders regarding that discontent. Such communication could translate into valuable corporate governance changes. In this regard, vote no campaigns provide shareholders with an indirect, but potentially potent, role in corporate affairs. On the other hand, that role does not undermine board authority and autonomy because the plurality system ensures that while the board may consider shareholder input, directors retain the discretion to determine board structure and corporate policies. Thus, vote no campaigns may represent an ideal balancing of shareholders' interests in influencing corporate affairs against the board's authority for managing those affairs.

Some evidence suggests that vote no campaigns do in fact achieve these goals. One recent study revealed "consistent evidence across a broad set of measures suggesting that on average [just vote no] campaigns are effective in spurring boards to act."[11] Professor Grundfest and others have cited this study not only as demonstrative of the impact of vote campaigns, but also to suggest that shareholders can impact corporate behavior even when their actions do not (and cannot) directly result in the removal of particular directors.

III. Walt Disney and the Majority Voting Movement

The 2004 director election at The Walt Disney Co. ("Disney") sparked considerable shareholder unrest with respect to the merits of plurality voting. During that election, shareholders organized a vote no campaign to express their dissatisfaction with Disney's then CEO and board chair Michael Eisner regarding the employment agreement and exit package he facilitated between Disney and its former president Michael Ovitz.[12] In 1995, Eisner had encouraged Disney's board to hire his friend Ovitz as Disney's president — the first time in its history that Disney had hired a president.[13] Unfortunately, Ovitz's tenure was short-lived. In fact, almost immediately after his hire, Ovitz's relationship with Eisner and Disney executives deteriorated, and eventually everyone agreed that Ovitz was not a good fit for Disney.[14] As a result, Ovitz only served as president for fourteen months; Eisner and the Disney board arranged for Ovitz to leave without cause.[15] Under the terms of his employment contract, such an arrangement entitled Ovitz to receive a $130 million severance package.[16]

The severance amount sparked shareholder outrage, particularly because the Disney board admitted that while it knew that certain stock awards would be accelerated at Ovitz's departure, the board was completely surprised that the acceleration would lead to such a large amount of money. Indeed, the board originally believed Ovitz's severance package could be as low as $15 million.[17] Several shareholder suits ensued, alleging, among other things, that the board had breached its duty in negotiating both Ovitz's initial contract and his severance.[18] After several years of litigation, the Delaware Supreme Court found that while Eisner and the board's conduct fell far short of best practices, it did not amount to a breach of duty.[19]

Shareholders' continued outrage spurred the 2004 vote no campaign against Eisner. Roy Disney, nephew of Walt Disney and son of a Disney co-founder, spearheaded the campaign. At the time, the campaign was one of the most successful in history, resulting in 45% of shareholder votes being withheld against Eisner, along with sizeable withhold amounts for other targeted directors.[20]

In shareholders' view, the success of the campaign highlighted the flaws with the plurality voting system, sparking a campaign to alter that system. Indeed, a plurality voting rule meant that even if shareholders had withheld more than 50% of their votes against Eisner, Eisner would have remained on the board. By contrast, shareholders believed that a majority vote system would have ensured that their vote had a realistic potential of removing Eisner from his chairmanship. In other words, shareholders believed that if corporations had a rule requiring that directors receive a majority of shareholder votes in order to be elected, then their votes would actually impact director elections. As a result, shareholders began advocating that Disney and other corporations adopt majority voting as a default rule in director elections.

Shareholders' campaign for majority voting began in earnest with the 2005 proxy season. In 2004, the year before the Disney election, shareholders submitted only twelve proposals urging corporations to adopt a majority voting rule.[21] In 2005, that number increased more than seven-fold to 89.[22] In 2006, shareholders submitted more than 150 majority vote proposals.[23] In fact, in 2006 shareholders submitted more majority vote proposals than any other shareholder proposal.[24] Shareholder support for such proposals rose from 12% in 2004 to 48% in 2006.[25] Thus, by 2006, and in just one short year, majority voting had become "the" shareholder issue of the proxy season. Resulting in part to increased adoption rates by corporations, 2006 represented the high-water mark in terms of the number of majority vote proposals.[26] However, shareholder support for majority voting proposals has increased over time. By 2008, average shareholder support for majority vote proposals had reached 50.2%.[27] In 2009, average support was up to 58%.[28]

The increased support for majority voting has translated into corporate adoption. At the start of 2005, less than one hundred companies had adopted a majority vote regime.[29] In sharp contrast, by June of 2008, 72% percent of S&P 500 companies and more than 60% of *Fortune* 500 companies had some form of majority voting regime in place.[30] As of July 2009, 77% of S&P 500 companies had some form of majority voting.[31] These statistics reveal that in just a few years, shareholders have managed to generate a virtual sea change in the director election standard.

IV. Majority Voting Regimes

The term "majority voting" encompasses a variety of different voting structures. As a general matter, such structures fall along two axis. The first can be classified as a "true" majority voting regime, pursuant to which nominees must receive a majority shareholder vote in order to be elected as a board member.[32]

The second structure has been referred to as a "plurality plus" regime. Under that regime, plurality voting remains the default rule. However, if a director fails to receive a majority of the vote, she must tender her resignation to the board, and the board has some period of time (usually 90 days) to determine whether to accept the resignation. Corporations that have adopted a plurality plus model often require that anyone elected as a director execute an irrevocable resignation to be effective upon their failure to receive a majority shareholder vote. Pfizer, Inc. ("Pfizer") developed the first plurality plus model. Pfizer believed that such a model enabled shareholders to have a greater impact over director elections, while guarding against failed elections and other problems associated with majority voting.

Although early adopters chose the plurality plus model, the true majority vote regime has now become more prevalent. In 2005, Disney became one of the first companies to adopt a plurality plus rule for its director elections. A little over a year later, Disney adopted a true majority vote regime. Consistent with this pattern, in 2006, most corporations opted into a plurality plus structure. Thus, by February 2007, 60% of companies had adopted a plurality plus regime, while only 39% had embraced a true majority voting rule.[33] However, by 2008, 49.5% of S&P 500 companies had a true majority voting system, while 18.4% had a plurality plus regime.[34] By July 2009, 59% of S&P 500 companies had adopted true majority voting, while only 18% had implemented plurality plus.[35]

V. Legislative Support

State legislators have responded to shareholders' majority voting campaign. Prior to 2006, nearly every state corporate code provided for plurality voting as the default rule in director elections.[36] However, by 2008, California, Nevada, North Dakota, Virginia, and Washington had amended their corporate code to permit corporations to make majority voting the default rule.[37] Some states have made efforts to support the plurality plus regime. Spear-heading such efforts, in 2006, the ABA's Committee on Corporate Laws amended the Model Act to allow shareholders or the corporation to implement a plurality plus regime through a bylaw amendment.[38]

Other states have made changes to facilitate the majority vote effort. In 2006, Delaware amended its corporate code to provide that the board cannot repeal a shareholder-adopted bylaw specifying the amount of votes a director needs to be elected.[39] This provision ensures that the board cannot unilaterally alter shareholder-adopted majority voting bylaws. Delaware also amended its corporate code to provide that a director's resignation can be effective upon future events or dates and conditioned upon the failure to receive a certain number of votes. Such contingent resignations can be made irrevocable.[40] These provisions effectively validate the kinds of resignations tendered pursuant to a plurality plus regime, and hence buttress the viability of that regime. The ABA and other states also have adopted such resignation provisions.[41]

Efforts to implement majority voting at the federal level were derailed. At least one version of Congress' 2009 proposed financial reform bill would have mandated majority voting for all public companies.[42] Legislators removed the mandate from the final bill.

VI. Broker Voting

As Chapter 2 reveals, many shareholders purchase their shares through a broker, relying on their brokers to cast their votes. SEC and NYSE rules require that brokers request instructions from shareholders regarding how they would like brokers to vote their shares. However, under NYSE Rule 452, if brokers do not receive instructions ten days prior to the meeting, they are allowed to vote shares held in their control without instruction, so long as the vote relates to matters designated as "routine." Historically, uncontested elections were deemed to be routine, enabling brokers to vote uninstructed shares in such elections.

More recently, shareholders began to criticize this kind of uninstructed voting because of its potential to distort election results in favor of management. Studies confirm that broker voting overwhelmingly mimics that of management.[43] Because brokers' uninstructed votes can be as much as 19% of the total vote, such votes could have a significant impact on director elections.[44] For example, broker votes would have changed the outcome of the Disney vote no campaign, resulting in a majority of votes being cast against Eisner.[45] This kind of evidence prompted shareholders to push for a rule change related to broker voting.

In July 2009, the SEC altered NYSE Rule 452 to eliminate un-contested elections from those matters deemed to be routine, elim-inating uninstructed voting in this arena.[46] In 2010, Dodd-Frank solidified this change, not only applying it to all national exchanges, but also extending the ban to advisory votes on compensation and any other matter the SEC deems significant.[47]

These changes to the broker voting rules could have a signifi-cant impact on majority voting and vote no campaigns. On the one hand, such changes could increase the relative success of vote no campaigns because they increase the likelihood that directors will receive a greater portion of withheld votes when shareholders target them in connection with vote no campaigns. On the other hand, such changes may make it more difficult for directors to gar-ner majority support in uncontested director elections, increasing the potential for directors to lose their seat. In addition, there is concern that the rule change could make it more difficult for com-panies to satisfy quorum rules. To address this concern, it is ad-visable that corporations include on their proxy statement routine matters such as voting for independent public accountants so that broker uninstructed votes can be counted for quorum purposes.

VII. Smoke and Mirrors?: Critics and Proponents of Majority Voting

Advocates of majority voting insist that it is necessary to ensure that shareholder votes impact election outcomes and corporate pol-icy. Such advocates criticize plurality voting because under such a system, directors could remain on the board despite significant share-holder dissent. Majority voting responds to this criticism, and thus appears to give shareholders greater authority over the election process.

By comparison, critics point out that strong vote no campaigns provide shareholders with this authority without the necessity of altering the plurality system. Ironically, Disney, the corporation that triggered the majority voting movement, may underscore this point. Indeed, as a result of the vote no campaign, Disney removed

Eisner as board chair within hours of the final vote tally. Six months later, Eisner stepped down as CEO and relinquished his board seat, though he insisted that his decision had no connection to shareholders' vote no campaign. Despite such insistence, these actions suggest that a vote no campaign can have a tremendous impact on board elections and corporate governance, not only when less than a majority of votes are withheld against a director, but also when a vote no campaign occurs in the context of a plurality voting system where such votes have no direct repercussions. From this perspective, the aftermath of the Disney campaign reveals that a vote no campaign can be effective without majority voting. Indeed, empirical evidence supports the notion that vote no campaigns have an impact on corporate conduct, and thus can be a significant vehicle for shareholders to have a voice in corporate affairs without resorting to a majority vote standard.

Critics also insist that majority voting could have an adverse impact on board structure. The departure of directors triggered by a majority voting rule not only could reduce the optimal mix of skills and expertise within the boardroom, but also could potentially result in the board failing to have sufficient directors who qualify as independent or who can meet financial literacy requirements under federal law.

Finally, at least two professors point out that majority voting as implemented "is little more than smoke and mirrors" because directors, rather than shareholders, continue to retain discretion over board elections.[48] State law provides that incumbent directors continue to hold their seats until a successor is duly elected.[49] This provision is referred to as the "holdover rule." The holdover rule is the safety valve for a failed election, ensuring that in the event a director fails to be elected, but there is no replacement director, the ousted director maintains his directorship. Thus, even in a true majority vote regime, the holdover rule means that directors who fail to receive a majority vote remain in office until a successor is secured. State law grants incumbent directors the authority to fill board vacancies. Hence, even if shareholders alter the holdover rule to require a director's immediate removal, generally boards, rather than shareholders, select the replacement. In a true majority voting regime, these rules ensure that directors, as opposed to shareholders, have the ultimate authority to determine the composition of the board.

Under a plurality plus regime, directors have even more discretion because they can determine if they will accept director resignation. Therefore, under either form of majority voting regime, shareholders' vote is not likely to end a director's tenure in office. Instead, in both cases, the incumbent board and management retain the authority to determine directors' fate, and hence the overall fate of the boardroom. In this way, the holdover rule greatly diminishes the distinction between a true majority voting rule and a plurality plus regime.

It also appears to greatly diminish shareholders' control over director elections. Existing evidence reveals that even with the changes in director voting rules, most directors remain in office despite strong shareholder dissent. In fact, although almost 100 directors failed to receive a majority vote in 2009, none of those directors relinquished their board seat. To the extent such dissents occurred under a plurality plus regime, the boards at issue did not accept director resignations. The one dissent that occurred in the context of a true majority vote system also resulted in the director retaining her seat. To be sure, this evidence may not reflect a failure of the majority vote system. Indeed, in some cases, strong shareholder dissent triggered enhanced communication between shareholders and directors, along with a satisfactory resolution of the issues prompting such dissent. In that regard, the fact that a director was not removed from the board may not necessarily signal the ineffectiveness of majority voting. However, it does highlight the considerable discretion incumbent directors and managers continue to have over board elections.

VIII. Future Trends

Although majority voting has become prevalent, it is by no means universal. Within the last few years, majority voting has become the dominant standard for director elections at large public companies. Yet there remain many large companies without majority voting regimes. Importantly, most corporations that have changed their director election standards are incorporated in Delaware.[50] Then too, the shift at large public companies is not being mirrored at smaller companies. As of December 2008, some 54% of Russell 1000 companies and 74% of Russell 3000 companies still employ plurality voting.[51] Moreover, as of July 2009, 86% percent of S&P 500 small cap companies still used plurality voting.[52] As these statistics reveal, while the majority voting campaign has experienced considerable success, there continues to be significant ground to cover, especially at smaller companies.

One law firm encouraged companies confronted with a majority voting proposal to consider "bowing to the inevitable" by sponsoring a majority voting rule, while urging companies that have not received such proposals to "seize the corporate governance high ground" by proposing such a rule.[53] Given this kind of continued support for majority voting, it is likely that shareholders will continue to make headway, and that majority voting may become nearly universal at larger companies. Consequently, shareholders likely will turn their attention to smaller companies in the next phase of their campaign.

CHAPTER 7

Proxy Contests and the Fight for Corporate Control

Proxy contests, or proxy fights, refer to the situation in which there is an attempt to elect directors who are not supported by management. Proxy contests potentially represent the most powerful tool shareholders can wield to influence corporate affairs, not only because such contests enable shareholders to replace existing directors, but also because they could lead to a change of control at the targeted company. Thus, shareholders' ability to wage or threaten to wage a proxy contest has the potential to alter the direction of a corporation. Given this potential, corporations devote considerable resources in response to threatened or actual proxy contests. Moreover, the prospect of a proxy contest often spurs the board to adopt some of the changes advocated by shareholders, or otherwise to more actively engage with their shareholder base. This chapter explores proxy contests and then examines some of the more prominent proxy fights in recent history.

I. The Nuts and Bolts of Proxy Contests

A. Proxy Contest Mechanics

A proxy contest occurs when a person or entity seeks to elect a set of directors different from those supported by management. This election battle is referred to as a proxy contest because when it occurs in a public company, it occurs through the proxy apparatus. The parties engaged in the contest solicit proxies from shareholders. Multiple proxy contests can be waged at the same time. In addition, there is no requirement that the person or entity waging the proxy contest be a shareholder of the targeted company. However, as a general matter proxy contests are waged either by existing shareholders or by someone who has accumulated stock in preparation for a proxy contest. Obviously the larger a shareholder's stake, the less support she needs to garner to be successful. For ease of discussion, this chapter will refer to those who wage proxy contests in opposition to management's slate as shareholders—though they are sometimes referred to as insurgents or dissidents.

Any proxy solicitation must comply with the federal proxy rules. Such rules require the creation of a proxy statement, which must be distributed to solicited shareholders and filed with the SEC. For corporations, the proxy statement must include information about the corporation and its business, including certain financial data, as well as information about the corporation's nominees. Soliciting shareholders must include information about themselves and their nominees.

The proxy statement also must include a proxy card. A proxy card is not a ballot, although it is sometimes referred to as such. Instead, a proxy card grants the soliciting shareholder the right to serve as proxy and cast a ballot on behalf of solicited shareholders. A proxy card not only must provide the solicited person with the ability to indicate that they are giving someone else authority to vote for a particular nominee, but also must provide solicited shareholders with the ability to withhold their proxy authority with respect to any director nominee.

In addition to matters associated with the director election, the proxy statement also must include any issue on which shareholders are required to vote. Typical issues included in the proxy statement are those involving selection of the company's public accountant and approval of shareholder proposals. When there are additional matters to be voted on, the proxy card must enable solicited shareholders to indicate whether they will grant authority to approve, disapprove, or abstain from voting with respect to each separate matter to be voted upon.

These requirements mean that when there is a proxy contest, shareholders receive multiple proxy statements and cards. Generally, shareholders will issue proxy cards in a particular color in order to distinguish their proxy cards from the corporation's and to reduce confusion associated with competing proxy cards and statements.

Notably, the proxy rules exempt solicitations that do not involve more than ten shareholders from the proxy solicitation definition. Such an exemption enables shareholders to engage in limited proxy contest without having to incur the expense of a proxy solicitation. For corporations in which institutional shareholders hold a sizable portion of the corporation's stock, this exemption can have a significant impact on shareholders' ability to wage a proxy fight.

The SEC is considering an amendment to the proxy rules that would allow a shareholder seeking to vote against a board's proposal on a particular matter to submit the board's proxy card with an instruction that the board vote against the proposal. Such an amendment would mean that shareholders could wage a campaign against the board's proposal without having to incur the expense of creating a proxy statement and card. Consequently, shareholder activists could encourage other shareholders to vote against a particular proposal, and those wishing to support the activists would be able to display their support by returning the board's proxy card to such activists. In essence, an SEC amendment on this issue could facilitate vote no type campaigns with respect to particular issues in the same manner as shareholders wage vote no campaigns against directors.

B. Proxy Contest Expenses

Proxy contests involve significant costs. The SEC estimates that the cost of printing and distributing the proxy statement is approximately $18,000.[1] However, proxy contests also involve the costs of hiring legal counsel to ensure that the proxy statement and solicitation process complies with federal securities laws, as well as costs associated public relations and advertising aimed at garnering support for director nominees. On average, proxy contests cost about $500,000. However, proxy contest expenses can range from tens of thousands of dollars to millions of dollars. One shareholder incurred $10.4 million in a proxy contest to secure board seats at

Six Flags.[2] Similarly, during a proxy contest for control of Lockheed Corp., shareholders spent $6 million, while the corporation spent an estimated $8 million.[3]

As a general matter, corporations pay all of the expenses associated with incumbent or management supported directors, while soliciting shareholders must pay their own proxy expenses. State law governs the question of whether corporations are required or entitled to pay anyone's proxy costs. That law allows corporations to reimburse the reasonable expenses associated with proxy contests. Importantly, management supported candidates rarely need to be reimbursed because the corporation often pre-authorizes funds to be paid on behalf of such candidates. Moreover, whether expenses are deemed reasonable only arises if shareholders challenge them. Not only do shareholders rarely challenge such expenses, but courts give corporations significant discretion in determining whether an expense is reasonable. The result is that in almost all circumstances, the corporation covers all of the proxy expenses incurred by management supported candidates.

By contrast, because state law does not require corporations to reimburse shareholders for their proxy expenses, it is rare for such reimbursement to occur. Importantly, there are no litigated cases involving shareholders seeking reimbursement after losing a proxy contest. Even for shareholders who are successful, cases generally impose two limitations on the reimbursement request. First, shareholder expenses must be reasonable. Second, shareholders must authorize the reimbursement—though in some cases courts have found that board authorization is sufficient. The practical effect of these rules is that shareholders almost never receive reimbursement for their proxy expenses, unless they are able to gain control of the board, and thus influence the corporation's reimbursement decision.

Increasingly, shareholders have used the shareholder proposal process to seek to alter this reimbursement regime. Thus, shareholders have submitted proposals aimed at encouraging corporations to adopt bylaws that would reimburse proxy expenses under certain circumstances.

In 2009, Delaware amended its corporate code to give corporations the ability to adopt bylaw provisions requiring reimbursement of shareholders' proxy expenses.[4] The Delaware code allows corporations to subject reimbursement to any lawful procedures or conditions they choose, including limits on the reimbursement amount and conditioning someone's eligibility for reimbursement on the number of persons nominated. The Delaware law is permissive, and thus does not require corporations to adopt reimbursement provisions.

However, in light of shareholder concern surrounding this issue, companies may decide to adopt such bylaw provisions. For example, in November of 2009, Healthsouth adopted an expense reimbursement bylaw pursuant to which a shareholder will be reimbursed for reasonable expenses incurred in connection with soliciting a single nominee so long as the nominee (a) qualified as an independent director, (b) was independent from the nominating shareholder, and (c) received at least 40% of the votes cast.[5]

C. The Rate and Success of Proxy Contests

Historically, proxy contests have been relatively rare. Despite the existence of thousands of public companies, one study found an average of 40 proxy contests a year.[6] Outside of takeover battles, that average dropped to 11 a year.[7]

The rarity of proxy contests stems from a variety of factors. First, proxy contests are costly. Second, often shareholders threaten a proxy contest, but never actually wage such a fight. Some shareholders threaten a proxy contest in order to gain the corporation's attention; such shareholders' primary goal is engagement rather than board representation. Third, the disruptive nature of proxy contests makes them unattractive. Fourth, proxy contests generate uncertainty regarding whether the shareholders' slate will be better equipped to manage and oversee the corporation than the existing board. Hence, even when shareholders are dissatisfied with the incumbent board, such uncertainty may make them reluctant to support the shareholders' slate. Such reluctance increases the likelihood of defeat, and thus decreases shareholders' willingness to conduct proxy fights. Ultimately, proxy contests are viewed as drastic, and thus a measure of last resort.

In recent years, shareholders have been more willing to wage proxy contests. From 2001–2005, shareholders engaged in an average of 61 proxy battles.[8] From 2006–2009, proxy contests reached record numbers, with each year surpassing the previous record. Thus, in 2006, shareholders waged 100 proxy fights, while waging 107 in 2007.[9] In 2009, shareholders waged 133 proxy fights.[10] The financial crisis and resulting recession has led to a decline in proxy fights.[11] However, these figures reveal that proxy contests rose significantly within the last decade.

In the last decade shareholders also have achieved unprecedented success in their proxy fights. Thus, from 2001–2005, shareholders' average success rate of a proxy contests was 45%, with success defined as shareholder activists obtaining at least one contested board seat.[12] The success rate in 2006 climbed to 57%, and reached 50% in 2007.[13] In 2008, the success rate hit a record high of 71%, and if settlements were counted, that rate would have been 80%.[14] In 2009, shareholder activists achieved success in 60% of the proxy fights that went to an actual vote.[15]

Success in relation to a proxy contest not only means securing seats after having engaged in a proxy battle, but also includes success through negotiated settlement agreements with the corporation pursuant to which shareholders gain some board representation. While settlement agreements are privately negotiated, and hence may differ significantly, they generally address several common factors. First, such agreements usually include a standstill agreement pursuant to which shareholders agree not to engage in certain actions for a period of time. Prohibited activities range from supporting or waging a proxy contest to restrictions on stock ownership. Second, the corporation will agree to support some (though generally not all) of the shareholders' nominees. Such an agreement also may include an agreement to appoint such nominees to particular board committees. Third, the corporation will agree not to nominate a number of its own candidates, particularly those who shareholders believed to be most objectionable. Fourth, the agreement generally will include the expansion of the board. Fifth, some agreements also provide for reimbursement of the shareholders' proxy expenses. Finally, settlement agreements may contain benchmarks that the corporation must meet. The corporation's failure to meet such benchmarks generally entitles shareholders to certain remedies, such as the ability to disregard the standstill agreement or otherwise gain the corporation's support for additional shareholder nominees to the board.

D. Short Slate Campaigns

Shareholders can engage in different kinds of proxy contests. They can wage a contest involving a full slate of directors or a slate of directors that would constitute control of the board. Alternatively, shareholders can wage a campaign that only seeks to elect a minority of the directors. This latter campaign is referred to as a "short slate" campaign. When a company's board is staggered, a shareholder's only option is to wage a short slate campaign to replace those directors whose staggered term expires at the annual meeting. However, when the entire board is up for re-election, shareholders have the option of running a full slate, control slate, or a short slate.

There are several advantages to a short slate campaign. First, because it does not involve a change in control, it may be easier for shareholders to get the support of their fellow shareholders. Second, and related to the first, short slate campaigns may be less expensive, particularly if shareholders only engage in limited solicitations. Indeed, many short slate campaigns only target specific shareholders and thus make use of the exemption for solicitations of less than 10 shareholders.

Historically, one drawback of a short slate campaign is that it could lead to situations in which shareholders could not or do not elect a full board. The proxy rules provide that no nominee may appear on a proxy card unless she has consented to be named in the proxy statement. The rule is known as the bona fide nominee rule. Because it is not likely that management-supported candidates will consent to be named in a shareholder's proxy statement, this rule meant that shareholders could not include the names of management candidates in their proxy statement. As a result, shareholders seeking to support the shareholder's slate would not have the opportunity to round out their slate by voting for a mix of shareholder and management-supported candidates on one proxy card. Then too, because the proxy rules provide that the last proxy card submitted by a shareholder supersedes any previously submitted card *in its entirety*, the proxy rules effectively prevented shareholders from submitting two proxy cards. In this respect, the proxy rules precluded shareholders from voting on a full slate of directors if they chose to support a shareholders' short slate campaign. This made the short slate campaign unattractive, thereby undermining its potential for success.

However, in 1992, the SEC adopted Exchange Act Rule 14a-4(d) to ameliorate this problem. Under Rule 14a-4(d), a shareholder can include the names of the management candidates for whom it will vote on its proxy card under the following circumstances: (1) the shareholder's solicitation must only involve a minority of the board; (2) management candidates and the shareholder candidates must collectively constitute the full slate of directors being elected; (3) solicited shareholders must be given the opportunity to withhold their vote with respect to any management nominee; and (4) the proxy card must state that there is no assurance that the management-supported nominee will serve if elected along with the soliciting shareholders' nominee. Importantly, Rule 14a-4(d) does not allow shareholders to vote for management candidates who are not supported by the soliciting shareholder. In other words, shareholders cannot split their votes in a manner different from what the soliciting shareholder has contemplated.

A shareholder can only create a different mix of candidates in two ways. First, if there is electronic voting, the competing parties can agree to let the service provider give shareholders such an ability. However, it is unlikely that the parties will consent to such a voting arrangement. Second, the shareholder can attend the annual meeting and vote on the manual ballots. An option that only will be exercised by the most dedicated and diligent shareholders.

The SEC is considering an amendment to the proxy rules that would enable shareholders to round out their proxy card by adding the names of nominees from other shareholder campaigns, in the same manner that they can round out their slates using the company's nominees.

E. Strategic Issues

Engaging in proxy contests involves important strategic considerations for both the company and soliciting shareholders. Timing is important for both parties, particularly in terms of when and how they communicate with shareholders. Moreover, both parties must consider how best to market their campaign and respond to issues raised by the other campaign.

Corporations also can seek to ward off proxy contests through advance planning. First, effective communication with shareholders may make shareholders more receptive to corporate actions during a proxy contest. Second, implementation of certain changes in the corporation's governance doctrines decreases shareholders' ability to wage a successful campaign, or at least to take control of the company's board. Most notably, classified boards undermine shareholders' ability to take control of a corporation in one election cycle. Of course, this fact has made such boards a target of shareholder activism. The success of such activism undermines corporations' ability to deter and fend-off proxy fights.

Third, corporations can institute shareholder rights plans, also known as poison pills. A poison pill grants shareholders the option either to purchase more of the company's shares at a discounted price or to purchase shares of an acquiring company's stock at a discounted price post-merger. Pursuant to the pill, shareholders' option to exercise their purchase right is triggered once a potential bidder acquires a certain percentage of the company's stock—typically 20% or more, and cannot be exercised by the bidder. Such options therefore dilute the bidder's interest, making it more difficult for the bidder to obtain sufficient shares to gain control of the company. As a result, the existence of a poison pill has one of two impacts. First, the pill encourages potential bidders to negotiate directly with the board because the board has the ability to redeem the pill. Such a negotiation slows down the takeover process while enabling management to obtain important concessions from bidders. Second, when negotiations break down or bidders are otherwise unwilling to directly engage with the board, bidders can bring a lawsuit against the corporation seeking to have the pill overturned. Courts have upheld the validity of poison pills, particularly when they are adopted to ward off future takeovers, and not adopted in reaction to a specific takeover attempt. In courts' view, a poison pill enables the board to consider whether takeover bids are in the best interest of the corporation and its shareholders, and hence reflects an appropriate exercise of the board's fiduciary responsibilities. Thus, unless a poison pill can be deemed unreasonable or the result of self-dealing by management, it generally will survive a bidder's challenge. Consequently, poison pills represent one of the corporation's most powerful weapons in the takeover battle.

Shareholders also must consider strategy when waging a proxy contest. One critical consideration involves deciding the type of contest to wage, which often depends upon the likelihood of success of the particular contest. Shareholders also must be mindful of any impediments to their contest. Such impediments include whether the company has a poison pill, and if so, determining the strategy for having the poison pill redeemed or withdrawn.

II. Some Notable Proxy Contests

A. Shaking Up Heinz—2006

The largest proxy contest of 2006 focused on the future of H.J. Heinz Co. ("Heinz"). The contest involved hedge fund manager Nelson Peltz, and his fund Trian Group. Peltz had a history of acquiring stakes in underperforming companies in the food industry with strong brand names such as Arby's and Wendy's, and working with management to enhance shareholder value. In particular, Peltz had made a name for himself with his successful turnaround of Snapple, which he purchased for $300 million in 1997, and then sold some three years later for $1 billion.

Peltz engaged in at least two strategic actions prior to waging his proxy contest. First, in February 2006, Peltz began accumulating Heinz stock. By the August 2006 annual meeting, Peltz held 5.5% of Heinz stock, making him the second largest Heinz shareholder.[16] Second, Peltz sought to engage with management. Thus, in March 2006, Peltz met with the Heinz CEO and outlined certain operational improvements he believed would enhance shareholder value. Peltz' primary concern was that Heinz's stock had declined 38% over the past eight years. Hence, Peltz insisted that the company needed to engage in various cost-cutting measures. During these discussions, Peltz requested that five candidates he supported be nominated to the board. Eventually, Heinz rejected Peltz's proposal and his request for board representation.

Thereafter, in May 2006, Peltz launched a proxy contest to gain five of the twelve board seats up for election at the August 2006 annual meeting. His slate included himself and four others. His proxy statement outlined a strategic plain aimed at enhancing shareholder value, including reducing costs by cutting administrative expenses and improving plant efficiency, reinvesting in marketing and production, and re-focusing on key brands. Peltz also proposed that the company increase its share repurchases and dividend payments.

In a seeming attempt to fend off Peltz, Heinz implemented several changes.[17] Thus, it reduced spending, issued a higher dividend and increased its share buyouts. It also adopted several corporate governance changes, including implementing majority voting procedures, cutting its supermajority provisions, and committing to hold regular meetings between independent directors and key shareholders. Finally, Heinz made a commitment to add up to two additional independent directors to the board. Peltz viewed these changes as a sign of his successful influence over the corporation.

The summer months before the contest included a war of words between Heinz and Peltz. Peltz continually insisted that the board was incapable of unlocking shareholder value. Heinz—through its website—responded in a variety of ways.[18] First, Heinz insisted that Peltz's plan set unrealistic targets that would cripple the company. Second, Heinz insisted that Peltz's nominees were unqualified and had close personal connections with Peltz that would prevent them from representing the interest of all shareholders. In particular, Heinz emphasized the fact that, if successful, Peltz, the owner of 5.5% of the stock, would control over 40% of the board. Third, Heinz contended that Peltz had a history of inappropriate conduct towards shareholders.

Despite these arguments, Peltz managed to secure two board seats.[19] Those seats included one for himself and another for former Snapple executive Michael Weinstein. Peltz's efforts were likely given a boost by support from RiskMetrics and two other proxy firms.

The Heinz board committed to working with Peltz, and it appears that their alliance has not been acrimonious. In fact, nearly a year after Peltz entered the Heinz board room, the company's stock jumped 34%.[20] By 2010, however, some investment experts purported to be underwhelmed by Heinz's performance.[21] At that time, Peltz had decreased his investment in the company to about 1.5%.[22]

B. Yahoo and the Battle for Search Engine Supremacy — 2008

The Yahoo!, Inc. ("Yahoo") proxy contest centered on a proposed combination between Yahoo and Microsoft, Inc. ("Microsoft"). Such a combination is designed to enable the companies to compete with the search engine and online advertising business of Google, Inc. ("Google"), which holds two-thirds of the search engine market.

The 2008 battle over Yahoo began with an unsolicited takeover bid from Microsoft. In February 2008, Microsoft offered to purchase all of Yahoo's outstanding shares for $31 a share, a 65% premium over its most recent closing price.[23] Less than two weeks later, Yahoo's board unanimously rejected the offer on the basis that it substantially undervalued Yahoo. In addition, Yahoo took steps seemingly aimed at undermining any efforts at a takeover attempt. Thus, Yahoo adopted an employee retention plan that would provide various equity awards to employees who were either fired post-merger or left as a result of a decrease in their responsibilities after a merger.[24] The plan could cost any purchaser an additional $2 billion to take over Yahoo.

Despite these actions, Microsoft announced its intention to launch a takeover, and thus make its offer directly to Yahoo shareholders, if Yahoo's board failed to accept its offer within three weeks. Microsoft also raised its offer to $33 a share—$4 shy of the $37 a share Yahoo directors claimed they were seeking. In the face of the Yahoo's board continued rejection, however, Microsoft formally withdrew its offer on May 3, 2008. Yahoo's actions displeased many shareholders.

On May 15, 2008, Carl Icahn, corporate raider turned shareholder activist, announced his intention to wage a proxy contest to replace Yahoo's entire 10-person board. Icahn's primary objective was to negotiate a merger between Yahoo and Microsoft. Icahn accumulated 4% of Yahoo's shares in preparation for the contest. Icahn's 10-person slate included himself, Harvard Law School Professor Lucian Bebchuk, and Dallas Mavericks owner Mark Cuban.

Several developments occurred in July 2008 that impacted the proxy contest. First, on July 7, Microsoft announced that it could not negotiate any deal with Yahoo if the officers and directors did not change. Second, Yahoo announced on July 12 that it had rejected another offer from Microsoft involving, among other things, Microsoft's acquisition of Yahoo's search engine business. According to Yahoo, the offer was unacceptable because it required the replacement of its existing board and top management. Finally, on July 18, Legg Mason, a 4% Yahoo shareholder, announced its intention to cast its shares in favor of Yahoo's slate of directors.

On July 21, Yahoo and Icahn entered into a settlement agreement related to the proxy contest. The agreement provided for eight members of the incumbent board to be up for reelection at the annual meeting. Following the annual meeting, the board would be expanded from 10 to 11 members. The remaining three director slots would be filled by Icahn and two members appointed from a list of nine candidates recommended by Icahn.

In addition to changes to the board, the proxy contest clearly had an impact on the company's direction. On July 30, 2009—

about a year after the contest—Yahoo and Microsoft entered into a 10-year partnership, granting Microsoft access to Yahoo's search technologies. In exchange, Yahoo is to receive 88% of search-generated advertisement revenue for the first five years of the partnership.[25] In October 2009, Icahn resigned from the Yahoo board, indicating that he believed that the company no longer needed an activist director. In November 2009, Yahoo's CEO and co-founder Jerry Yang announced that he would step down from his position as CEO, but remain on the board. In February 2010, the merger between Yahoo and Microsoft was officially approved, putting the companies in a position to compete with Google.

This proxy contest is notable not only because it involved Microsoft—the world's biggest software company—but also because it could have a profound impact on the search engine market.

C. Targeting Target—2009

Beginning in 2007, William Ackman, founder of the hedge fund Pershing Square Capital Management, L.P. ("Pershing Square"), launched a campaign focused on Target, Inc. ("Target"). In connection with his campaign, Ackman established a separate fund, Pershing Square IV, for the exclusive purpose of holding Target stock. Ackman's fund accumulated 9.6% of the common shares of Target.[26]

Ackman sought at least two specific changes at Target. First, he wanted to encourage Target to sell its credit card operations. Between 2003 and 2006, most other large retailers had sold their credit card operations for substantial sums of money. Importantly, many analysts believed that such operations could be risky because of the deteriorating credit market and the increased frequency of delinquent or lack of credit card payments.[27] Target insisted that its credit card operations represented an integral part of its retail business, and hence resisted the trend towards selling such operations. Ackman was vocal in his belief that Target's resistance in this area was inappropriate, and undermined the company's ability to enhance its financial profile. The second change advocated by Ackman focused on a shift in the company's real estate strategy. Target owned 85% of its stores and the land beneath them, the most of any big box retailer.[28] Ackman believed Target could sell its real estate holdings in a manner that would increase shareholder value.

Initially, Ackman sought implementation of these changes by engaging with Target's management. Ackman began pressuring Target to sell the credit card business in the summer of 2007. By September of 2007, Target had begun evaluating a potential sale of its credit card operations, and in May of 2008, Target sold 47% of those operations to JP Morgan Chase for $3.6 billion.[29] Although Target insisted that Ackman's actions had not impacted these transactions, most people viewed them as a sign of Ackman's influence over Target. Ackman also sought to influence Target's real estate strategy. In October of 2008, Ackman announced a proposal aimed at gaining value from Target's real estate. When Target responded by pinpointing various defects with the proposal, Ackman revised the proposal. However, Target rejected the amended proposal.

Ackman then launched a proxy contest.[30] The contest included a dispute about how many directors were up for reelection. Historically, Target had a board of 13 directors, elected through staggered terms every three years. However, one director resigned in January of 2009, and Target announced that it would not fill the vacancy, but instead shrink the board to 12 directors. As a result, Target insisted that only four directors would be elected in 2009. Because Target's charter indicated that only shareholders could decide to shrink the board, Ackman insisted that five directors should be up for election. Ultimately, Target included a proposal on the proxy statement requesting shareholders to decrease the board size to 12. Importantly, if shareholders rejected Target's proposal, at least one of Ackman's nominees would have secured a board seat. In the end, Ackman nominated five candidates, including himself, while Target's slate contained four incumbent directors. Target and Ackman collectively spent $21 million dollars on the proxy contest.[31]

Proxy advisors issued conflicting advice about the Target contest. Proxy Governance and RiskMetrics recommended that shareholders approve two of the five people nominated by Ackman.[32] Glass Lewis recommended that shareholders approve Target's slate.[33]

At the meeting, shareholders voted overwhelmingly in favor of Target. At least 70% of the voted shares approved Target's incumbent directors, as well as the proposal to decrease the board size to 12.[34]

Interestingly, the fight encouraged Target to more actively engage with its shareholders. Indeed, Target's CEO revealed that he had reached out to fifty of Target's investors since the proxy fight began.

Although Target successfully thwarted the proxy contest, many viewed the fight as a significant turning point in shareholder activism. Indeed, Target was one of the largest companies to ever be involved in a proxy fight. In addition, it was one of the most high profile campaigns in many years. Moreover, at the time of the fight, Target was relatively well-respected with no record of poor governance. Hence, the fight suggested that no company was immune from shareholder activism and proxy battles.

D. The Next Chapter for Barnes & Noble—2010

The 2010 battle over Barnes & Noble, Inc. ("Barnes & Noble") involved determining the future of the nation's largest book store, and its strategy for turning the relatively unprofitable traditional book business into a business that could compete in an electronic market. Importantly, as with other bookstores, Barnes & Noble's stock had been in decline for years. Moreover, the company reported significant first quarter losses in 2010. Although Barnes & Noble entered into the electronic reader business with the launch of its e-reader Nook, it faced heavy competition from Amazon.com, whose Kindle e-reader enabled the company to hold about 70% of the e-book market. In fact, at least one analyst downgraded Barnes & Noble's stock to underperform in September 2010 based on concerns that its electronic-based strategy faced significant challenges from entities such as Amazon.com.

Billionaire investor Ronald Burkle's bid for Barnes & Noble appeared to begin as an attempted hostile takeover of the company. Burkle first purchased Barnes & Noble shares in 2008 through his company Yucaipa Companies. At that point, Barnes & Noble's founder and chairman Leonard Riggio was also its largest shareholder, holding 29% of the company's stock. When Barnes & Noble launched the Nook in October 2009, Burkle disagreed significantly with Riggio regarding the company's strategy surrounding the e-reader. Seemingly as a result of this disagreement—and in antic-ipation of a potential takeover—in November of 2009, Burkle increased his stake in the company to 16.8%. In response, Barnes & Noble adopted a poison pill limiting shareholders to a 20% stake in the company. In August 2010, Burkle purchased sufficient shares in the company to increase his stake to just under 20%, making him the second largest Barnes & Noble shareholder. Burkle then filed a lawsuit to challenge the validity of the poison pill. Soon thereafter, Barnes & Noble put itself up for sale. Although Burkle and Riggio entered into negotiations to settle their disagreements, those negotiations broke down. Moreover, Burkle lost his suit sur-rounding the validity of the poison pill.

As a result, Burkle launched a proxy battle for the three board seats up for election at Barnes & Noble's 2010 annual meeting. Burkle's slate included himself and two other candidates. Burkle also requested that shareholders remove the poison pill. In his so-licitation to shareholders, Burkle insisted that the Barnes & Noble board's "failure to act independently of the Riggio family's agenda has contributed to the company's poor stock performance" and en-riched the family at the expense of stockholders.

In a letter to shareholders, Barnes & Noble pinpointed several rea-sons why they should reject Burkle's slate.[35] In particular, the com-pany accused Burkle of seeking to "gain creeping control" of the company by working with another investor, Aletheia Research Man-agement ("Aletheia"), to take control of the company without pay-ing a premium to shareholders. Aletheia was the third largest shareholder behind Burkle. Collectively Burkle and Aletheia owned about 35% of Barnes & Noble's shares. Barnes & Noble noted that the two companies had a history of investing together, including their collective ownership of 60% of the shares in A&P, Inc., the parent company of several supermarkets, including Super Fresh and Food Emporium. Burkle insisted that the companies were not working together. However, in its communication to shareholders Barnes & Noble pointed out language from the Burkle lawsuit, in which the court stated that the Barnes & Noble board "had good reason to be concerned that the two large investors were capable of and interested in cooperating in a joint effort to take effective control of the company." In addition, Barnes & Noble argued that Burkle had no strategic plan for the company and its future, but instead had a record of being involved in some of the largest corporate failures in history.

Eight days before the meeting, Burkle won the support of Risk-Metrics, which argued that Burkle's slate could potentially improve the company's performance, while enhancing the board's independence and thereby undermining Riggio's influence.[36]

Ultimately, Burkle lost the proxy contest, but it was a close call.[37] The company's slate secured 52.5% of the shares present at the meeting, while 52% of the shares rejected Burkle's proposal to remove the company's poison pill.

In the aftermath, Barnes & Noble's future remains unclear. The board insists that it is still in discussions about a possible sale of the company or some other strategic alternative, including a potential merger with Borders Group, Inc. With respect to its financial health, while Barnes & Noble lost $75 million in the first half of 2010, it experienced a rebound during the holidays and recorded its biggest sales day in its history on December 23, 2010.

CHAPTER 8

BEYOND THE ANNUAL MEETING: ADVANCEMENTS IN SHAREHOLDER COMMUNICATIONS

Shareholder communications encompasses two forms: (1) communications among shareholders and (2) communications between shareholders and the corporation. Both forms can have a significant impact on shareholders' ability to influence corporate affairs. Shareholders who can effectively communicate with one another have a better chance of coordinating their efforts in a way that advances their concerns within the corporation. Historically, however, communications among shareholders in public corporations has been rare. Most attributed this rarity, at least in part, to the fact that public shareholders comprised a large group of dispersed individuals, and consequently did not have sufficient resources or opportunities to effectively communicate with one another. However, changes in the shareholder landscape coupled with legal and technological changes have greatly enhanced shareholders' ability to communicate with one another.

Corporate governance experts have long recognized that effective dialogue between shareholders and the corporation can be extremely advantageous to the corporation. First, such dialogue may be valuable simply because it allows shareholders to interact with the corporations, and thus gain confidence that the corporation has taken their views into account. In this respect, the dialogue generates a positive reputation for the corporation. Second, such dialogue promotes shareholder understanding of corporate policies and practices, potentially avoiding shareholder discontent that could cause shareholder activists to target the corporation. Third, corporate communication with shareholders not only can enable the corporation to gain a better understanding of shareholder concerns, but also gives corporations the opportunity to address those concerns as they arise. Finally, by providing shareholders with a vehicle for expressing their concerns, corporations may reduce shareholders' reliance on other more drastic measures of expression. Outside of the annual meeting, there are very limited opportunities for shareholders and corporations to meaningfully interact. To some extent, shareholder activism, including reliance on shareholder proposals, withhold the vote campaigns, and even proxy contests, reflects shareholders "knock on the door" at companies perceived to ignore shareholder concerns.[1] In this regard, shareholder communication may be one critical response to shareholder activism.

To be sure, communication between shareholders and the corporation poses special challenges. This is because ineffective communication could feed into shareholder discontent, promote misunderstandings, accelerate activism, and even trigger corporate liability. Given the potential for communication to alienate shareholders or otherwise produce these kinds of negative results, many corporations have steered clear of active engagement with their shareholders. Thus, despite technological changes that increase the opportunities for enhanced communications, communications between corporations and shareholders outside of the annual or special meeting remains rare for most public corporations.

This chapter discusses some of the factors impacting shareholder communications. It then concludes with some tips regarding how corporations can best avoid the pitfalls associated with ineffective dialogue with their shareholders.

I. The Role of the Institutional Investor in Effective Communication

The fact that institutional shareholders comprise the bulk of the modern shareholder class enhances shareholders' ability to communicate. The historical presumption was that individual shareholders' relative dispersement posed difficulties for effective communications. However, institutions are able to overcome such difficulties. First, institutions can devote the resources necessary to facilitate better interactions with other shareholders and the corporation. Second, it is relatively easier for corporations to identify and communicate with institutions than with a large group of dispersed shareholders. Third, when corporations reach out to institutions, they are able to engage with shareholders who hold a significant portion of shares, and hence who both individually and collectively hold significant voting power, making communications with institutions more efficient and effective.

Fourth, institutional shareholders' concentrated ownership facilitates their ability to communicate within a particular corporation and across corporations. This is particularly true with respect to the nation's top corporations because a relatively small number of institutions hold a sizable share of such entities. For example, in 80% of the top 25 largest US corporations, ten institutions hold 20% or more of the company's stock, with some institutions holding more than 30% of company stock.[2] Those same ten institutions also own significant stock in most of the top 25 corporations.[3] These ownership patterns increase the likelihood that institutional shareholders can more easily and effectively communicate with one another.

Importantly, while interacting with institutional investors is essential for facilitating effective shareholder communications, corporations should not ignore their retail shareholders. Some corporations have a large retail shareholder base. Moreover, some retail shareholders have played a significant role in shareholder activism, and hence communications with them is also important, though it may prove more difficult than engagement with institutions.

II. Proxy Regulations and Effective Communication

Proxy solicitation rules have a direct impact on shareholders' ability to communicate with one another. Federal rules require that before shareholders can engage in a proxy solicitation, they must register proxy disclosure documents with the SEC.[4] The creation and filing of such documents involves considerable cost. The SEC and courts interpret proxy solicitation broadly to include any communication that could result in the attainment, withholding, or revocation of a proxy. This interpretation raises the concern that communications could be viewed as a proxy solicitation, subjecting them to costly registration.

In 1992, the SEC sought to alleviate this concern and thus facilitate shareholders' ability to more freely communicate.[5] The SEC adopted a rule effectively exempting shareholder communications from the proxy solicitation definition so long as such communications did not include a request to act as someone's proxy. By exempting such communications, the 1992 rule increased the likelihood that shareholders could consult and act cooperatively with one another. Empirical evidence reveals that shareholder communications increased significantly after the rule's adoption, and thus that the rule did in fact serve to enhance shareholder engagement.

III. Electronic Shareholder Forums

The SEC's 2008 rules on electronic shareholder forums aimed to enhance shareholder communications on the Internet. Electronic shareholder forums are essentially platforms that allow communications through the Internet.[6] Such forums can take many forms, including a bulletin board, a website that allows for the posting of questions and answers, or a blog. In adopting the 2008 rules, the SEC pinpointed two hurdles to shareholders' use of Internet-based forums: (1) the cost of complying with the proxy rules if communications made on a forum are considered proxy solicitations, and (2) concerns that anyone who operates a forum will be liable for statements made by forum participants.[7] The 2008 rules sought to remove these two hurdles. First, the rules exempted certain communications made in an electronic forum from the proxy solicitation definition. Solicitations on an electronic shareholder forum are exempt so long as they are not designed to obtain a proxy, and they occur more than sixty days prior to the date of a company's announced annual or shareholders meeting (or more than two days after an announcement is made about a meeting to occur in less than sixty days). Second, the rules make clear that those who host an electronic shareholder forum are not liable for statements made by third parties participating in the forum—though hosts remain liable for their own statements.

The SEC hoped that the rules surrounding electronic shareholder forums would facilitate better communication among shareholders, and between shareholders and companies. For shareholders, such forums not only provide a cost-effective means of communicating on a more routine basis, but also could serve as a vehicle for shareholders to coordinate their actions. Also, if corporations host electronic shareholder forums, then such forums expand shareholders' opportunities to interact with the corporation throughout the year, rather than being limited to interactions during the annual or special meeting. For corporations, hosting an electronic shareholder forum could enable companies to gain insight regarding shareholder views on critical issues. Such forums also enable corporations to monitor and respond to shareholder concerns as they arise.

However, in addition to liability concerns, there is concern that such forums could have limited utility. With respect to shareholders, rather than serving as a platform for serious discussion about significant policy concerns, such forums could become little more than chat rooms. Or worse, such forums could be used to generate negative publicity and information about a corporation. With respect to corporations, it is possible that corporations could limit their use of such forums to marketing of positive information about the company, rather than as a vehicle to engage in a two-way dialogue with shareholders.

To date, it is unclear whether and to what extent electronic shareholder forums have proved beneficial. Many shareholders as well as several large corporations have created electronic shareholder forums. However, there is little data on the number of such forums or the extent and nature of their use.

IV. The Influence of the Internet

The Internet has the potential to be a powerful tool in facilitating shareholder communication. Indeed, the Internet provides a cost-effective way for shareholders to engage with one another. In recent years, shareholders have used websites, emails, Twitter accounts, and other electronic media not only to monitor corporate behavior, but also to encourage other shareholders to participate in specific campaigns.

Yahoo experienced the influence of the Internet firsthand. In 2007, Eric Jackson, the owner of 45 shares of Yahoo stock, used various electronic media outlets, including a blog, wiki, and videos on YouTube to encourage other shareholders to join his campaign to change the direction of Yahoo. His campaign included the creation of a website where shareholders could contribute ideas for "Plan B"—a plan aimed at proposing strategic changes at Yahoo, including removal of then Yahoo CEO Terry Semel, along with changes to the company's governance policies and practices.[8] The Plan B website garnered support from 150 shareholders representing about 3.5 million shares of Yahoo stock.[9] Such supporters, known as the Plan B group, were the first group of shareholders assembled through the Internet with the purpose of impacting corporate governance changes. In 2007, Jackson not only submitted Plan B to Yahoo managers, but also attended the annual shareholders' meeting on behalf of the Plan B group to advocate for implementation of the Plan B changes.[10] Semel stepped down several days later, and many attributed his departure to the awareness raised by Jackson's online activities. Jackson also led an online withhold the vote campaign against three Yahoo directors that ultimately garnered 31% of the shareholder vote.[11] Jackson's efforts demonstrate how even shareholders with relatively small stakes in a company can use the Internet to communicate with other shareholders and ultimately impact corporate affairs.

Corporations also have taken advantage of communication through the Internet. Electronic forms of communication represent a potentially powerful method to enhance communication between corporations and shareholders because they are cost-effective, reach a broad audience, and enable the corporation to have more routine interactions with shareholders.

Every major corporation has a website that it uses to post information, including a specific webpage devoted to investor relations aimed at providing critical information to shareholders. Many corporations also have blogs and Twitter accounts. A 2008 study revealed that 16% of *Fortune* 500 companies host public blogs.[12] Three of the top five *Fortune* 500 corporations have blogs, while 38% of the top 100 have corporate blogs.[13] Ninety percent of corporations who host blogs allow the public to submit comments to the blog, thus providing a mechanism for ongoing dialogue between the corporation and its shareholders.[14] Corporations also have used Twitter accounts to interact with investors, posting information about the company and its financial health. For example, several companies have held Twitter sessions to report quarterly earnings, while others, such as WalMart and Johnson & Johnson, have held Twitter sessions in connection with their annual meetings. Corporations use such sessions to disseminate information on a range of topics from revenue results to strategic developments.[15] Blogs and other forms of electronic media help facilitate ongoing communication between shareholders and the corporation.

Corporations that use the Internet to communicate with shareholders must ensure that they comply with federal securities laws. Rule 10b-5 of the Exchange Act ("Rule 10b-5") prohibits corporations from making material misstatements or omissions.[16] Companies must ensure that any information they disseminate complies with this rule. This means that companies must monitor their electronic media to ensure that posted material does not become stale. Companies also must be cautious with respect to any hyperlinks made available on their sites because such links expose companies to liability when the information contained in them can be perceived as endorsed by or attributable to the corporation. Companies must be particularly mindful when using Twitter because the brevity of the communication on Twitter not only increases the likelihood that corporations will use shorthand that can be misinterpreted, but also makes it more difficult to include disclaimers that could protect corporations from liability related to particular statements.[17]

V. Regulation FD

Regulation Fair Disclosure, known as Regulation FD, is aimed at preventing corporations from selectively disclosing information in a manner that could result in insider trading. Adopted in 2000, Regulation FD requires that when a public company or someone acting on its behalf discloses material non-public information to market professionals or securities holders who may trade on the information, the company must simultaneously disclose that information to the public.[18] Regulation FD applies to corporate communications made during shareholder meetings if there are no media involved and the meeting is not broadcast by electronic means. It also may apply to Internet communications such as blog posts or Tweets if those communications can be viewed as the dissemination of non-public information to select shareholders. Thus, companies must be mindful of the type of information made available on the Internet and to whom the information is provided.

There is concern that Regulation FD has had a significant impact on corporations' willingness to openly communicate with shareholders. On the one hand, studies suggest that corporations fear that communications with select shareholders could result in disclosure of material information and therefore violations of Regulation FD.[19] On the other hand, some shareholders and regulators fear that corporations use Regulation FD to avoid communicating with shareholders.

Seeking to respond to these fears, the SEC provided interpretive guidance on Regulation FD in June 2010.[20] That guidance clearly stated that Regulation FD does not prohibit corporate directors and officers from speaking privately with shareholders or a group of shareholders. However, the SEC did indicate that corporations should pre-clear discussion topics with counsel to insure that such topics did not constitute material non-public information. In addition, the SEC noted that even material non-public information can be provided to select shareholders when the shareholders expressly agree to keep the information confidential. It is unclear whether and to what extent Regulation FD is a deterrent to dialogue between shareholders and the corporation. But it is clear that corporations seeking to engage in dialogue with particular shareholders must be mindful of the implications of such dialogue for purposes of Regulation FD.

The SEC has stated that corporations can use the Internet to comply with Regulation FD's requirement of simultaneous dissemination of information. Hence, information posted on a company website can be viewed as public if the website is sufficiently broad-based, it is posted in a manner that is generally available to the securities market, and there is a reasonable time to digest the posting.

VI. Increased Activism

Increased shareholder activism has encouraged corporations to reach out to their shareholder class. Much of shareholder activism reflects shareholders' attempt to express concern about corporate performance and other important issues. In this regard, better communication with shareholders is an essential part of the response to shareholder activism. Such communication enables corporate directors and officers to demonstrate that they are aware of, and seeking to tackle, shareholder concerns. It also promotes understanding between the corporation and shareholders, which could enable corporations to avoid being the target of activist campaigns.

In light of increased shareholder activism, corporations have taken a variety of different steps aimed at enhancing their interaction with shareholders. Thus, some corporations have arranged meetings with shareholders who engage in activism, particularly those who submit or plan to submit shareholder proposals, those who threaten withhold the vote campaigns, or those who threaten to wage proxy contest. Other corporations have established regular mechanisms for receiving and processing shareholder concerns through the Internet. For example, Microsoft started a blog in 2009 and invited shareholders to communicate their corporate governance concerns on the blog.

Many companies host conference calls designed to explain their financial statements, and some investors have requested additional calls with corporations. Indeed, companies routinely hold quarterly earnings conference calls to discuss their financial results for the quarter. The calls are generally available to the public through the Internet or some other electronic media, and include prepared remarks from company officers lasting about thirty minutes, followed by a brief question and answer period. In 2010, a group of institutional investors led by Walden Asset Management requested that several companies host a conference call for institutional investors to focus on corporate governance issues that arise within the proxy statement.[21] This "Fifth Analyst Call" would occur after the company had issued its proxy statement but before the annual meeting, and would be designed to enable investors to raise questions and concerns about the company's corporate governance philosophy and strategy prior to the annual meeting.

Still other corporations have pledged to meet with their large shareholders on a more routine basis. In 2007, Pfizer was the first corporation to announce an intention to meet with its largest shareholders. Pfizer invited thirty of its largest shareholders, who collectively represented 35% of the Pfizer shareholder base, to meet with the board and discuss the corporation's governance policies and practices, including executive compensation. The meeting agenda and discussions were kept confidential. A few other corporations also engaged in such meetings, including Bristol-Myers Squibb, Goldman-Sachs, Home Depot, McDonald's Corp., Occidental, Schering-Plough, and UnitedHealth Group.

While Pfizer's actions reflect an effort by some corporations to increase communications with shareholders, their actions continue to represent the exception rather than the rule. Studies reveal that very few corporations have face-to-face meetings with shareholders outside of the annual and special meetings.[22] As a consequence, many corporations' sole interaction with shareholders occurs in the context of a problem or crisis. Corporate governance experts and corporate managers alike recognize that this style of corporation-shareholder communication is problematic, failing to take advantage of the potential benefits associated with effective communication, including the possibility that such communication can decrease the potential of being targeted by discontented shareholders.

Shareholder activism also has impacted engagement with retail shareholders. Recent actions such as changes to the broker voting rule and the reliance on electronic proxy voting, have had or could have a negative impact on retail shareholder participation. Thus, after the implementation of e-proxy, there was a significant decline in retail shareholder participation. There is also concern that changes in the broker voting rules will disenfranchise retail shareholders who neglect to provide voting instructions related to key issues. This has prompted corporations and regulators to develop ways to better interact with retail shareholders in order to insure their continued engagement in the voting process.

VII. Some Critical Planning

While increased communication between corporations and shareholders may prove beneficial, it also could have negative repercussions. Effective dialogue therefore requires appropriate preparation from corporations. As an initial matter, corporations should consider their approach to shareholder communications more generally. Corporate governance experts indicated that such consideration should involve the following issues:

- Development of a board-shareholder communication policy, including the manner in which shareholder inquiries will be handled
- Attainment of legal guidance on any constraints associated with shareholder communication
- Gaining an understanding of the shareholder base and any changes to that base
- Determination of the types of issues most appropriate for board or management level response
- Identification of the areas of most concern to shareholders

- Development of a system for tracking and reporting the results of any shareholder communication

Some corporations have sought to meet privately with shareholders either on a more routine basis or as a result of some specific issue or campaign raised by the shareholder. These private meetings also require careful planning. In conducting such meetings, corporate governance experts suggest that the following should be considered:

- Development of policies and procedures to govern the private meeting
- Pre-clearance of any topics to be discussed at the meeting with management, the board, and corporate counsel
- Consideration of whether corporate counsel should be present at the meeting
- Identification of the appropriate shareholder representatives to participate in the meeting
- Identification of the appropriate corporate officers and/or directors to participate in the meeting
- Sufficient preparation of any corporate participants, including understanding of any legal issues involved with such a meeting

VIII. The Road Ahead

Changes in the shareholder landscape, coupled with legal and technological changes, have greatly enhanced shareholders' opportunities to communicate with one another and the corporation. Shareholders have taken advantage of these opportunities to engage in more robust communication on a more routine basis. While corporations have used electronic media to increase their communication with shareholders, face-to-face meetings outside of traditional platforms continue to be relatively rare. As long as corporations can adopt appropriate shareholder communication policies, the future likely will bring expanded corporate efforts to engage in more effective communication with their shareholders on a more routine basis.

CHAPTER 9

PROXY ACCESS: THE FINAL FRONTIER?

I. The Proxy Solicitation Hurdle

Most shareholders of public companies vote by proxy.[1] As Chapter 2 reveals, this means that shareholders convey their particular voting preferences to another person, and then authorize that person to cast a ballot with those preferences on their behalf. Given the dispersed nature of public shareholders, voting by proxy ensures that shareholders can vote without having to attend a shareholder meeting, while simultaneously ensuring that enough shareholders are deemed present to satisfy quorum rules. Because most public company voting is conducted by proxy, whenever shareholder approval is needed for a particular matter, including the election of directors, shareholder proxies must be solicited.

Federal proxy rules prohibit any entity or individual from soliciting proxies without first filing a proxy statement containing information related to the subject matter of the solicitation with the SEC, and distributing that statement to solicited shareholders.[2] Thus, with respect to director elections, a proxy statement identifying and providing information about director nominees must be filed with the SEC and distributed to shareholders.[3] The proxy statement also must contain a proxy card on which shareholders can designate an agent to serve as their proxy and indicate their voting preferences.[4] In light of the proxy rules, public corporations distribute a proxy statement and proxy card each year when seeking to elect board members. Because the proxy rules apply to all proxy solicitations, shareholders who desire to solicit proxies for director candidates of their choice also must distribute a proxy statement and proxy card to shareholders.

Historically, the federal proxy rules have allowed corporations to exclude the names of shareholder-nominated candidates from the corporate proxy statement. Rule 14a-8 allows shareholders to make "proposals"—recommendations or requirements that the company take certain actions—that the corporation must then place on the corporate proxy statement so that they can be voted on at the shareholder meeting.[5] However, historically Rule 14a-8(i)(8) enabled corporations to exclude shareholder proposals related to director elections.[6] In light of this rule, the corporate proxy statement only included the names of nominees supported by management.

In light of the proxy rules, if shareholders desired to nominate their own candidates for director, they had three alternatives, all of which were relatively unappealing. First, shareholders could recommend candidates to the board and convince the board to place such candidates on the corporate proxy statement. Empirical evidence suggests that management rarely embraced shareholder recommendations related to director candidates.[7] Second, shareholders could attend the annual meeting and nominate director candidates from the floor of the meeting. However, the fact that most shareholders vote by proxy not only means that most shareholders do not attend the annual meeting in person, but also means that most shareholders cast their vote prior to the annual meeting date. Hence, proxy voting undermines the extent to which shareholder attempts to nominate director candidates at the annual meeting can result in the actual election of such candidates.[8] Third, shareholders could distribute their own separate proxy statement. Empirical evidence suggests that the costs— both monetary and logistical—associated with creating and distributing proxy materials make a separate solicitation prohibitive for all but a select few shareholders.[9] The relative unattractiveness of these three alternatives underscores the fact that most shareholders did not have realistic avenues for nominating directors of their choice.

II. The Proxy Access Debate

Faced with these alternatives, shareholders repeatedly have sought to obtain proxy access—the ability to access the corporate proxy statement for purposes of nominating candidates of their choice. Shareholders contend that the lack of proxy access not only undermines the effectiveness of their voting power, but also undermines their ability to influence corporate affairs and hold directors and officers accountable for their behavior.

As an initial matter, shareholders insist that the lack of proxy access significantly curtails their nomination and election rights. Shareholders rarely nominate director candidates.[10] This rarity may be a function of rational shareholder apathy or even shareholders' basic content with the status quo. Yet shareholder activists contend that this rarity stems from the limited options available for effective shareholder nominations. Regardless of its roots, the fact that shareholders rarely nominate director candidates has at least two consequences. First, most directors are nominated only by the incumbent board and management. Second, most directors run without opposition. Shareholder activists contend that such a structure makes elections a pre-determined event pursuant to which shareholders merely ratify the choices of the incumbent board and management. From this perspective, shareholders have argued that the lack of proxy access renders their vote virtually meaningless.

Because shareholders' vote reflects the primary means by which shareholders can influence corporate affairs, shareholder activists also insist that the lack of proxy access undermines the strength of that influence. Courts have made clear that shareholders cannot interfere with officers' and directors' broad authority to manage the affairs of the company.[11] Electing directors not only enables shareholders to have an indirect voice in the day-to-day decisions of the company, but also helps ensure that directors (and those who serve at their pleasure) feel accountable for those decisions. However, if elections are pre-determined by directors, then shareholders' role in this process is diminished, decreasing the likelihood that such elections will serve as a mechanism for enhancing the extent to which directors and officers feel accountable for the decisions they make. In this respect, because it minimizes shareholders' role in the election process, shareholder activists contend that the lack of proxy access reduces the likelihood that directors will pay heed to shareholder concerns, while undermining shareholders ability to play a role in preventing managerial shirking and misdeeds. Importantly, shareholder activists view proxy access as the "holy grail" of shareholders' rights because it appears to have the greatest potential to strengthen their voting rights and thereby strengthen their ability to effectively oversee the corporation and its managers.[12]

Shareholder agitation for proxy access often peaks when officers and directors engage in fraud or other misdeeds that appear to highlight the lack of effective accountability measures. On the heels of the corporate and accounting scandals of 2002, shareholders vigorously complained that the lack of proxy access denied them the meaningful ability to oversee corporate affairs. The SEC reviewed the proxy rules because of concern that those scandals stemmed from a lack of appropriate accountability.[13] Similarly, in 2009, the SEC's decision to reconsider the viability of proxy access resulted from "serious concerns about the accountability and responsiveness of some companies and boards of directors to the interests of shareholders" raised by the economic crisis and recession.[14]

Opponents of proxy access raise several concerns. First, opponents insist that proxy access will increase the number of proxy contests. Such an increase may prove costly to shareholders because corporations could waste valuable time and resources in combating those contests.[15] Such an increase also may serve to discourage qualified candidates from serving on the board, undermining the quality of the boards as a whole.[16]

Second, opponents express concern that proxy access will enable shareholders with special or limited interests to have undue influence over the corporation and its affairs. On the one hand, proxy access will enable shareholders with relatively small stakes in the corporation to be a nuisance. On the other hand, proxy access will enable shareholders with relatively large stakes to engage in self-dealing, pursuant to which they will attempt to advance their own personal agenda to the detriment of the broader shareholder class and the corporation as a whole. There does exist empirical evidence suggesting that some shareholders engage in activism in order to pursue personal goals at odds with the broader shareholder class and the corporate interest as a whole.[17]

Third, opponents insist that shareholders are at an informational disadvantage relative to directors, and hence are not best positioned to make decisions about director nominees. This informational disadvantage makes proxy access unattractive because it could result in the selection of directors who lack expertise and other qualities necessary to elect a functioning board.

Finally, many insist that proxy access will not improve corporate performance or otherwise prevent abuses of authority. The empirical impact on the effect of shareholder activism on corporate performance is mixed at best, undermining the presumption that such access will improve the corporation's bottom line.

III. Proxy Access: The Fifth Time Is the Charm?

Shareholder agitation, coupled with the SEC's acknowledgment of shareholders' limited range of choices for nominating director candidates, has prompted the SEC to propose a proxy access rule at least five times.[18] In previous years, the SEC abandoned its proposal in the face of intense opposition. Despite similar opposition, in August 2010, for the first time in its history, the SEC adopted proxy access rules mandating that every public company grant proxy access to its shareholders, and that every public company allow its shareholders to propose additional proxy access models. Before describing the newly implemented rule, this section will look back at the historical attempts to implement proxy access.

A. Take One

In 1942, the SEC proposed a proxy access rule for the first time. The proposal would have given minority shareholders "an opportunity to use the management's proxy material in support of their own nominees for directorships."[19] Although the rule would have mandated proxy access for all public corporations, a company would not have been required to include more than twice as many candidates on the proxy statement as director positions to be filled.[20]

Intense opposition to the proposal convinced the SEC to abandon it.[21] Critics argued that the rule was unworkable. Their primary complaints were that shareholders would nominate unqualified candidates, and that shareholders would nominate too many candidates, thereby creating confusion among shareholders regarding how best to fill out their proxy cards.[22]

B. Take Two

In 1982, the SEC made a second attempt to implement proxy access rules. That attempt was stimulated by a series of roundtables hosted by the SEC in 1977 aimed at re-examining the proxy rules.[23] In connection with those roundtables, the SEC requested comments on a number of issues, including whether shareholders should be given access to the corporate proxy statement for the purpose of nominating candidates of their choice.[24] Based on those comments, the SEC proposed a rule that would have enabled a corporation, with the approval of its shareholders, to opt out of the federal shareholder proposal rules and adopt alternative procedures governing the process of submitting such proposals, including procedures governing the submission of director election proposals.[25] The SEC expected that these alternative procedures, at a minimum, would contain eligibility criteria and the bases for exclusion of any proposals.[26] In this regard, the SEC's proposal did not mandate proxy access; instead, the proposal would have enabled each corporation and its shareholders to determine whether to permit proxy access, and under what circumstances.

While there was some limited support for the proposal, most commentators expressed significant concern about the rules workability. Indeed, commentators argued that the proposal would be difficult to administer because there would be no "uniformity or consistency" in the proxy access procedures, if any, developed by companies.[27] Ultimately, the SEC made changes to the proxy rules, but abandoned its proxy access proposal.

Nevertheless, the SEC remained concerned about the relationship between proxy access and the effectiveness of shareholders' nomination right. In fact, one new rule implemented as a result of the 1977 roundtables required companies to indicate whether they had a nominating committee, and if so, whether such committee considered shareholder recommendations for director candidates. The SEC staff believed that such a rule, coupled with corporations' increased reliance on nominating committees, could obviate the need for proxy access by providing shareholders with an alternative channel for nominating candidates of their choice on the proxy statement.[28] However, the SEC staff indicated that it would revisit questions concerning the necessity of proxy access if nominating committees failed to appropriately consider and recommend a sufficient number of shareholder-supported candidates.[29] Importantly, a review of proxy statements for the 1988 proxy season found that only 55% percent of companies gave any indication in the proxy statement that they accepted director candidates from shareholders.[30] The review also revealed that many companies either had no established procedures for assessing those nominees or had procedures that likely deterred shareholders from making such nominations.[31]

C. Take Three

In 2003, the SEC proposed yet another proxy access rule. Enron and other corporate scandals of 2002 had generated significant concern regarding board accountability and the inability of shareholders to effectively oversee corporate activities.[32] Moreover, the SEC acknowledged that the increased presence of nominating committees had not provided shareholders with a meaningful voice in the director nomination process.[33] In the SEC's view, proxy access appeared to provide "the most direct and effective method" of giving shareholders a role in the director election process, and thereby indirectly giving them a role in overseeing corporate conduct and potentially preventing corporate misbehavior.[34]

As a result, the SEC proposed new Rule 14a-11 of the Exchange
Act ("Rule 14a-11"), granting proxy access to shareholders (alone
or as a group) who had continuously held at least 5% of a company's voting stock for two years after the occurrence of one of two
trigger events.[35] Under the first event, shareholders would be granted
proxy access in any election subsequent to the one in which more
than 35% of shareholders withheld their votes from at least one of
the company's director nominees.[36] The second event occurred if a
proposal requesting that a company be subject to proxy access as proposed under Rule 14a-11 was (a) submitted by a shareholder or
shareholder group holding more than 1% of the company's voting
securities for at least one year, and (b) received more than 50% of
the shareholder vote.[37] In other words, the second trigger event related to situations in which a majority of shareholders had recommended that a board approve a proxy access proposal, but the board
ignored that recommendation. The SEC believed these triggers sig-
naled evidence of a company's unresponsiveness to shareholder
concerns, and hence revealed the need for enhanced shareholder
participation in the corporate governance process.

After requesting comments on proposed Rule 14a-11, the SEC
made no effort to implement it, effectively abandoning the proposal without comment.

D. Take Four

In 2007, the SEC revisited proxy access. The SEC's decision was
prompted by the Second Circuit case of *AFSCME v. American International Group, Inc.* ("AIG").[38] In that case, AFSCME, an AIG
shareholder, sought to include a shareholder proposal on AIG's
proxy statement that would amend AIG's bylaws to establish procedures for granting proxy access to shareholders under certain circumstances. AIG argued that the proposal was excludable under
Rule 14a-8(i)(8), which prohibited shareholder proposals if they
related to an election. The Second Circuit noted that the issue was
complicated not only by the ambiguity of Rule 14a-8(i)(8) itself,
but also by the SEC's conflicting interpretations of the rule. The
SEC's first interpretation of Rule 14a-8(i)(8) was published the

same year the SEC adopted the rule. Under that interpretation, the SEC reasoned that shareholder proposals governing election procedures were not excludable under Rule 14a-8(i)(8) because such proposals would not result in an immediate election contest—and thus did not relate to an election. According to the Second Circuit, the SEC consistently applied this interpretation for fifteen years. However, the SEC gradually applied a second interpretation allowing companies to exclude election procedure proposals under Rule 14a-8(i)(8). The exclusion was based on the theory that proposals involving election procedures created a process for shareholders to create an election contest in the future, and thus related to an election for purposes of Rule 14a-8(i)(8).

Confronted with these differing interpretations, the Second Circuit reasoned that greater deference should be given to the SEC's first interpretation, not only because that interpretation coincided with the rule's implementation, but also because the SEC had not provided a rationale for changing its interpretation of the rule.[39] As a result, the Second Circuit found that proxy access proposals designed to establish procedural rules governing elections were not excludable under Rule 14a-8(i)(8). The Second Circuit concluded its opinion by suggesting that the SEC clarify its position with respect to Rule 14a-8, as well as its position regarding whether shareholders should be granted proxy access.[40]

In 2007, the SEC reanalyzed the proxy access issue in light of the *AFSCME* decision.[41] Importantly, the SEC proposed two conflicting rules. One rule would amend Rule 14a-8 to make clear that Rule 14a-8(i)(8) applied both to shareholder proposals related to director elections and to shareholder proposals related to *procedures* governing director elections.[42] The alternative rule would amend Rule 14a-8(i)(8) so that shareholders could propose bylaw amendments establishing procedures for granting proxy access to shareholders.[43] Shareholders could take advantage of the new rule only if shareholders (or a shareholder group) (1) had held more than 5% of the company's voting securities for at least one year, and (2) were not intending to change control of the company.[44] Shareholders submitting proposals would be free to craft any procedures they chose so long as the procedures did not conflict with state law, a company's bylaws, or a company's charter. Thus, the revised Rule 14a-8(i)(8) would give shareholders the flexibility of determining the terms under which they would be granted proxy access.

After receiving comments on the conflicting proposals, the SEC opted to deny shareholders proxy access. The SEC amended Rule 14a-8(i)(8) to clearly exclude shareholder proposals related to director election procedures.[45] The SEC insisted that allowing proxy access proposals under Rule 14a-8 would circumvent the proxy rules related to election contests, particularly rules governing required disclosures for such contests.[46]

E. Take Five

In July 2009, the SEC again proposed proxy access rules.[47] Unlike previous years, those proposed rules were eventually converted into final rules. Thus, in August 2010, the SEC adopted proxy access rules for the first time in its history.[48]

Similar to 2003, the SEC created a new Rule 14a-11 mandating proxy access for all public corporations. New Rule 14a-11 does not permit companies to opt out or otherwise limit its reach.[49] Unlike 2003, the new Rule 14a-11 does not subject the proxy access right to the occurrence of trigger events. Instead, shareholders are granted access to the corporate proxy statement so long as they (a) have owned at least 3% of the company's voting securities for at least three continuous years, and (b) do not seek a change of control of the company.[50] The maximum number of candidates who can be nominated to the board under Rule 14a-11 is one, or the number of candidates that represent up to 25% of the board, whichever is greater. Once the maximum number of candidates is elected to the board, shareholders cannot use Rule 14a-11 to access the corporate proxy statement. Thus, if there are existing directors who were nominated pursuant to Rule 14a-11 and their service continues past the election cycle, then those directors would count against the maximum threshold.

The corporation can exclude any nominee who does not meet objective independent requirements to which the company is subject. However, the candidate need not satisfy subjective independence requirements imposed by federal regulation or the company's governing documents. In addition, a nominee does not have to be independent from the shareholders who nominated him or her, although the rules require disclosures related to any relationships between a director nominee and the shareholder who nominates him or her.

Despite significant concern about the potential for abuse, the rules apply even if a company is confronted with a proxy contest. The rules prevent submitting shareholders from engaging in such a contest or otherwise acting in concert with shareholders engaged in a proxy fight.

The 2010 rules also alter Rule 14a-8(i)(8) to allow shareholders to propose bylaw amendments addressing procedures for proxy access. Importantly, the new rules do not simply amend Rule 14a-8(i)(8), but instead completely revise the rule. The new rule provides that a proposal related to director elections can only be excluded if the proposals:

- Would disqualify a nominee who is standing for election;
- Would remove a director from office before his or her term expired;
- Question the competence, business judgment, or character of one or more nominees or
- directors;
- Seek to include a specific individual in the company's proxy materials for election to the board of directors; or
- Could otherwise affect the outcome of the upcoming election of directors.

Hence, new Rule 14a-8(i)(8) overturns the proxy rules implemented in 2007. Importantly, the new Rule 14a-8(i)(8) does not supplant Rule 14a-11, nor can it be used to limit the proxy access rights granted under Rule 14a-11. Instead, Rule 14a-8(i)(8) represents an additional mechanism for shareholder access to the corporate ballot. Moreover, if state law rules provide a proxy access mechanism, that mechanism will not supplant Rule 14a-11, but will serve as an additional avenue for proxy access.

In adopting the proxy access rules, the SEC indicated that its primary objective was to facilitate the effective exercise of shareholders' state law right to nominate and elect directors. The SEC maintained that one of the core tenets of the federal proxy rules was to ensure that the proxy process "functions, as nearly as possible, as a replacement for an actual in-person meeting of shareholders." From this perspective, the proxy access rules were designed to remove federal law obstacles related to shareholders' state law election right.

Opponents of the new proxy access rules raised several concerns along the lines of the issues pinpointed in Section II of this chapter. In addition, opponents contended that mandated proxy access was inappropriate because whether companies grant proxy access should be a matter determined exclusively by agreement between shareholders and the corporation. This private ordering argument maintains that federal mandate of proxy access undermines shareholders' ability to freely choose the voting structure under which they will be governed. In this respect, Rule 14a-11 limits shareholders' rights by imposing a "one size fits all" voting rule that may not be appropriate for all shareholders and all companies. As a result, opponents of the new rules argued strenuously for the ability of shareholders and companies to opt out of the rules.

In adopting the proxy access rules, the SEC called the arguments based on private ordering flawed. As an initial matter, the SEC pointed out that some rights "cannot be bargained away," and that there were many instances in which both state and federal law mandated limits on private ordering. The SEC also insisted that the net effect of the rules would be to expand shareholder choice by providing them with an enhanced opportunity to nominate and elect a greater number of director candidates. Additionally, the SEC contended that a private ordering approach not only could be costly to implement because it had to occur on a company-by-company basis, but also that such an approach involved significant obstacles that could undermine shareholders' ability to effectuate their choices.

Prior to the enactment of the new rules, several corporations and commentators challenged the SEC's authority to mandate proxy access. In the SEC's view, when Congress adopted the federal proxy rules it recognized that voting through the proxy was a matter of federal concern, and hence the SEC believed such a challenge to be without merit. Importantly, in direct response to the challenge, Congress specifically enacted a provision in Dodd-Frank authorizing the SEC to craft proxy access rules.[51] As a result, the SEC maintained that any challenge in this area was moot.

The new rules were scheduled to take effect on November 16, 2010. Companies who mailed their proxy statement on or after March 15, 2010 would be subject to Rule 14a-11 for the 2011 proxy season. All other companies would not be subject to Rule 14a-11 until the 2012 proxy season. Smaller companies were given a three-year grace period before they were required to comply with the Rule 14a-11. In October 2010, the Business Roundtable and the US Chamber of Commerce challenged the new rules. The SEC opted to halt implementation of the rules until the courts resolve the challenge. Thus, as this book goes to press, it remains unclear whether, and under what circumstances, shareholders will be granted proxy access.

The new rules generate important questions about whether and to what extent shareholders will use proxy access, as well as whether and to what extent such access will impact director elections or corporate behavior. Given the importance shareholders place on proxy access, providing them such access is expected to have a dramatic impact on shareholders' ability to influence corporate affairs. Such access is also expected to have a dramatic impact on the corporate governance environment and corporate interactions with shareholders.

Comparison of Recent Proxy Access Proposals and Final Rule

Year	Rule 14a-8(i)(8)	Rule 14a-11	Share Ownership	Holding Period	Restrictions on Board Seats
2003	Proposals related to Rule 14a-11 proxy access procedures cannot be excluded	Proxy access for all public companies subject to trigger events related to the failure to implement majority voting or withholding of votes from directors	5% of voting stock	2 years	No intent to change control
2007	Proposals related to procedures for proxy access cannot be excluded	NONE	5% of voting stock	1 year	No intent to change control
2009	New rule; supplement Rule 14a-11; New rule that only allows specified exclusions	Mandated proxy access for all public companies	Sliding scale: 1% for large accelerated filers; 3% for accelerated filers; 5% for non-accelerated filers	1 year	Greater than one director or 25% of seats; priority determined on first-come basis
2010 Final Rule	Revised rule prohibits election-related proposals only if they meet specified requirements	Mandated proxy access for all public companies; smaller issuers delayed implementation	3% of voting power	3 years	Greater than one director or 25% of seats; priority determined by shareholder with largest holding

CHAPTER 10

INTERNATIONAL PERSPECTIVE ON THE EFFECTIVENESS OF INCREASED SHAREHOLDER POWER*

I. Shareholder Democracy around the Globe

Recent efforts to increase shareholder voting rights are not unique to the United States. Shareholders, as well as other institutions, have sought to enhance their voting rights in many other countries. This section begins with an analysis of the majority vote in other regions to provide a point of comparison. This section then assesses shareholder efforts to eliminate block voting, adopt a "one share, one vote" rule for corporations, and institute "say on pay." This section concludes with a brief examination of shareholder activism in general, to provide a more robust picture of shareholder efforts in other countries to increase their power.

A. Majority Vote Revisited

The quest for majority voting in the United States does not have a counterpart in most other countries, because the United States is unique in its application of the plurality standard. Indeed, most other developed markets already have a majority vote standard for director elections.[63] While the standards differ slightly, most countries embrace a default rule enabling shareholders to elect directors by majority vote. In the United Kingdom, the board appoints directors. Shareholders, however, must approve director appointments at the next annual general meeting, and their approval must be by a majority of shareholder votes.[64] Almost all other countries that have adopted or inherited an English-based legal system similarly have adopted a standard that allows shareholders to elect directors by majority vote.[65] In France, companies have either a unitary or two-tiered board structure. In French companies with a unitary board, not only must directors (excluding employee representatives) be elected by majority vote of the shareholders, but any votes in abstention are counted as votes against a director's election.[66]

In some countries, including the Czech Republic, Germany, Poland, and Russia, two-tiered board systems are the norm.[67] Under these systems, there is both a supervisory board and a management board.[68] Members of the supervisory board (other than employee representatives) are elected by a majority vote of shareholders, while the management board is comprised of directors appointed by the supervisory board.[69] Hence, when compared to most other voting systems, the American plurality system is an anomaly. As a result, the considerable shareholder activity related to majority voting in the United States has not been mirrored in most other markets.

As in the United States, however, majority voting has recently emerged as a critical governance issue in Canada.[70] Thus, in the last two years, institutional investors have mounted a campaign to alter Canada's plurality voting standard by working with dozens of boards to convince them to adopt a Pfizer-like director resignation policy for those directors who fail to get a majority vote from shareholders.[71] As a result of their efforts, more than half of Canada's sixty largest corporations adopted a director resignation or plurality plus policy during the 2006 proxy season.[72] As of June 2007, at least seventy-two Canadian corporations and trusts had adopted such a policy.[73] Mimicking the activism in the United States, Canadian investors have not only increased their efforts to dismantle the plurality vote rule, but many Canadian companies have responded by altering their governance rules to be more compatible with a majority vote standard.

Along similar lines, shareholders in Japan have been active in their efforts to maintain the ability to remove directors by majority vote. In Japan, like in most other countries, shareholders can elect directors by majority vote.[74] Prior to 2006, however, it took a two-thirds shareholders' vote to remove directors.[75] In May of 2006 a new Japanese corporation law became effective permitting the dismissal of directors by a simple majority vote.[76] In response to the law, several corporations have sought to restore the previous two-thirds standard by seeking shareholder approval to amend their by-laws to revert back to the old default rule.[77] Yet Japanese investors launched efforts to oppose such changes at all of the companies where amendments were attempted.[78] While not always successful, such efforts were notable, given the apathy often displayed by many Japanese shareholders.[79] Certainly, the change in Japanese law reflects a change aimed at strengthening shareholder voting power. More importantly, Japanese shareholders' efforts to maintain such a change indicates a sign of increased activism on the part of such investors.

B. Blocking "Share Blocking"

Shareholders in other countries have also finally managed to gain some ground on efforts to eliminate share blocking. In many continental European countries, including France, Italy, and the Netherlands, shareholders who wish to vote at an annual meeting must deposit their shares several days before the meeting.[80] Such shares are then effectively blocked from trading from the time of the deposit until the day of the meeting. This practice, known as "share blocking," is prohibited by American law, under which corporations cannot block shares before a shareholders' meeting.[81] Instead, corporations determine the eligibility of voters by establishing a record date.[82]

Share blocking has been characterized as a critical barrier to the exercise of shareholder voting rights. Indeed, opponents of share blocking believe it weakens voter turnout, particularly for foreign investors, who would rather abstain from voting than risk giving up their liquidity.[83] As one analyst notes, share blocking serves as a powerful deterrent to voting for institutional investors.[84] Ultimately, opponents argue that by promoting lower voting participation rates, share blocking weakens companies' incentives to be accountable to shareholders.[85]

Investors have long challenged this system. Indeed, activist investors have for many years sought to encourage corporations to voluntarily abolish share blocking.[86] Moreover, for several years, institutional investors and corporate governance groups have submitted proposals to the European Commission urging it to prohibit the practice of share blocking among member states.[87] Despite these efforts, the practice persisted, while the European Commission remained silent on the issue.

Now, however, that silence has been broken. In 2005, Germany amended its corporate law to require that German companies abolish share blocking and transition to the adoption of a twenty-one-day record date system.[88] After several public consultations, in June 2007, the European Commission adopted a shareholder rights directive requiring corporations to abolish the practice of share blocking in favor of establishing a record date for voting.[89] Corporations have two years to comply with the directive.[90]

These changes are viewed as enhancing shareholders' voting rights. Indeed, analysts believe the abolition of share blocking will spur greater voter participation, particularly among foreign investors.[91] Moreover, these changes exemplify the progress being made to enhance shareholder democracy in Europe.

C. "One Share, One Vote"

Although there is considerable disagreement about its utility, investors in various countries have encouraged corporations to adopt a "one share, one vote" rule. One share, one vote is a principle requiring that votes be allocated in proportion to the number of shares an investor holds. The NYSE and other U.S. listing agencies require that companies listed on their exchange adopt a one share, one vote rule.[92] As a result, one share, one vote is the norm in the United States. Advocates argue that the rule is not only democratic, but represents the optimal voting structure.[93] Many companies in other countries, however, do not have such a rule in place. For example, a recent study found that more than thirty percent of the companies included in the FTSE Eurofirst 300 index deviate from the one share, one vote principle.[94] The countries with the most deviation include France, the Netherlands, and Sweden.[95] The deviation stems from the adoption of various voting structures, including multiple voting rights as well as voting rights ceilings (where there is a cap on the number of shares an investor can vote, regardless of the number owned).[96] These and other practices ensure that investors do not get the benefit of the one share, one vote rule in many countries around the globe.

To be sure, there is disagreement about the importance of such a rule to shareholder rights. Indeed, one study concluded that the rule was not justified by economic efficiency.[97] Another study reached similar conclusions.[98]

Despite this disagreement, there has been renewed activity and focus around the issue of one share, one vote. Investors as well as the European Commission have pressured corporations to embrace such a rule.[99] Moreover, many companies have voluntarily adopted the rule.[100] While the transition to one share, one vote is uncertain, the increased attention on instituting such a rule reflects another example of shareholder efforts to protect and strengthen their voting rights in other countries.

D. "Say on Pay" Revisited

Shareholders in other countries have also zeroed in on executive compensation. Indeed, although executive compensation has not risen as dramatically in other countries as it has in the United States, executive salaries around the globe have gone up in recent years.[101] Moreover, investors in other countries have expressed sharp criticism regarding the apparent lack of connection between executive pay and company performance.[102]

Interestingly, as with majority voting, considerably more progress has been made in other countries with respect to "say on pay" than in the United States. In 2002, the United Kingdom became the first country to require a shareholder advisory vote on board pay.[103] Thus, U.K. shareholders had been casting a non-binding vote on compensation for almost five years before shareholders in the United

States even began agitating for such a vote. Although the vote is not binding on U.K. companies, it gives shareholders an opportunity to express their opinion on compensation practices at their firms. U.K. law also requires disclosure on various compensation data.[104] Other countries have followed the U.K. example. For instance, corporations in Australia and Sweden also must allow their shareholders to cast a non-binding vote on compensation.[105] Moreover, in Australia, one company had its remuneration report rejected by shareholders, while reports at several other companies received against votes as high as forty percent.[106] In contrast to those in Australia and the United Kingdom, corporations in the Netherlands must grant their shareholders a binding vote on executive compensation.[107]

These shareholder votes on compensation represent part of shareholders' ongoing struggle to curb compensation levels, and to ensure that executive compensation is more closely linked to performance. Furthermore, they reflect shareholders' quest for a greater voice in corporate affairs.

E. Shareholder Activism

Shareholders around the globe have demonstrated increased activism over the last few years, an activism that is in sharp contrast to the apathy that many such shareholders previously exhibited.[108] This activism underlines the general push for shareholder democracy, as well as shareholders' efforts to have a greater role in corporate affairs.

For example, shareholders in Japan have revealed unprecedented activism over the last few years. Indeed, studies confirm that most shareholders in Japan traditionally tended towards significant apathy.[109] This apathy was epitomized by the fact that historically, relatively few shareholders attended annual shareholder meetings.[110] In fact, the percentage of investors present at shareholder meetings had been decreasing steadily.[111] This lack of attendance had a significant impact on shareholders' ability to exercise their voice within Japanese corporations. Indeed, because of the relatively weak market for corporate control and other non-legal factors, experts believe that shareholder involvement at annual meetings represents one of the few ways in which shareholders can express their discontent with Japanese companies and play an active role in corporate governance.[112]

Shareholders' ability to play a role in shareholder meetings has been limited in at least two critical ways. First, the vast majority of Japanese companies hold their annual meetings on the same day, severely limiting activist shareholders' ability to participate in multiple shareholder meetings.[113] Second, and perhaps most problematic, the ability of shareholders to participate in shareholder meetings is undermined by the presence of sokaiya.[114] Sokaiya are essentially corporate extortionists who attend shareholder meetings on a company's behalf in order to quell any shareholder discontent and keep the meetings short—preferably under thirty minutes.[115] Apparently, corporations that do not agree to hire a sokaiya are subject to threats, intimidation, or worse.[116] One study revealed that some seventy-seven percent of Japanese corporations had admitted to paying sokaiya, even though such payments are illegal under Japanese law.[117] In fact, the rationale behind holding shareholder meetings on the same day was to limit the ability of sokaiya to police the bulk of such meetings.[118] Despite this rationale, uniform annual meetings and the presence of sokaiya combine to severely impede shareholders' ability to participate in meetings. This impediment underscores the general apathy historically displayed by investors in Japan.

Over the past few years, however, such investors have begun actively participating in annual meetings. Indeed, one study found that not only have meetings run longer than the traditional thirty minutes, but there also has been a rise in the number of shareholders attending meetings, as well as in the number of questions being asked at the meetings.[119] Moreover, shareholders have submitted more proposals at meetings. Thus, almost thirty companies faced shareholder resolutions in 2006, double the number facing such resolutions in 2005.[120] Some commentary suggests that this increased activism is due to an increase in the proportion of foreign investors.[121] Indeed, foreigners currently account for some twenty-eight percent of Japanese firm shares.[122] Foreign investors' willingness to be more involved in shareholder meetings has apparently spurred Japanese shareholders to do the same.[123] Given the importance of activism at shareholder meetings, the recent trend of greater involvement suggests that shareholders in Japan are beginning to play a greater role in corporate affairs.

Similarly, shareholders in Germany have displayed an increased level of activism. Like their Japanese counterparts, German shareholders historically have exhibited significant apathy.[124] Some contend that this apathy stems from the heightened role that banks play in the German proxy system relative to other countries.[125] In the last few years, however, Germany has witnessed an astonishing rise in shareholder activism.[126] Shareholder activists have mounted campaigns challenging a variety of governance practices, and have played a critical role in takeover battles at German companies.[127] Moreover, shareholders have been active in challenging directors and CEOs deemed to be underperforming.[128] These challenges are epitomized by shareholders' success in ousting the head of Deutsche Börse in 2005.[129] While many in Germany bemoan the recent rise in shareholder activism, that rise reflects shareholder efforts to gain a greater voice within German corporations.

In the United Kingdom, shareholder activism among institutional investors also has increased. Traditional shareholder activism has been rare in the United Kingdom.[130] Recent studies, however, reveal that shareholders, particularly institutional investors, have begun taking a more active role in governance affairs.[131] This increased activism is demonstrated by increased investor opposition to company resolutions, which has grown steadily in recent years.[132] In addition, a 2006 study revealed that U.K. shareholders have played an active role in replacing CEOs and board chairs, participating in restructuring decisions, and altering investment and company policies.[133] The study noted that this high level of shareholder engagement was distinct from previous periods, when shareholders rarely played a role in governance matters.[134] The study also found that such engagement yielded positive returns for shareholders.[135]

Some of the recent activism in the United Kingdom has likely been spurred by investors' ability to provide an advisory vote on executive pay. Analysts maintain that the mandatory shareholder vote has contributed to shareholder activism by increasing the level of dialogue between investors and company management.[136] Both the required vote and increased shareholder participation in issues of executive compensation reflect the growing levels of shareholder democracy within the United Kingdom.

While not all of the increased activity has yielded results, experts agree that heightened activism represents a new worldwide phenomenon. Hence, like their U.S. counterparts, shareholders in other countries have been pushing for a greater role in corporate affairs, and have subsequently used that role to press for change in the corporate structure.

II. Shareholder Democracy, An International Perspective

A. Shareholder Democracy and Passivity

Professor Stephen Bainbridge and other scholars have argued that shareholders' natural and rational apathy may undercut the extent to which they will use the power granted to them.[142] Studies by Professor Bernard Black and other scholars suggest that shareholders tend to be relatively passive, failing to exercise the voting power provided to them or otherwise engage in activism.[143] This relative passivity makes it unlikely that shareholders will benefit from increased power. Such an assessment gives opponents of shareholder democracy comfort, while suggesting that proponents' efforts in this area are in vain.

On the one hand, experiences in other countries would appear to confirm the view that shareholders' natural apathy will limit the extent to which they exercise any increased power they receive. For example, consider the practice of majority voting, the norm in most modern markets outside of the United States. Majority voting does not appear to have resulted in significant shareholder power in countries that observe it. To the contrary, shareholders do not appear to have used their vote to challenge directors. Thus, studies demonstrate that instances in which shareholders challenge managers' selections for directors are exceedingly rare.[144] This is true even in corporations that have been rocked by scandal. Moreover, this is true despite the fact that, unlike America, most other countries make it relatively easy to nominate alternative candidates for directors.[145] To be sure, cultural and other non-legal hurdles may explain the relative passivity of shareholders in other countries.[146] Studies suggest, however, that the crux of the problem may be relative apathy among shareholders.[147] Thus, experiences in these other countries appear to confirm the assertion that expanding shareholder democracy may have relatively little impact on the corporate governance landscape. Given that majority voting represents the signature campaign in the quest for increased shareholder democracy in the United States, these experiences do not bode well for advocates of increased shareholder power.

On the other hand, there is some evidence to suggest that shareholders may exercise their increased power in more subtle ways; hence, enhanced shareholder power may in fact have a greater influence on corporate affairs than theories about apathy would predict. Because it strengthens the impact of a withhold-the-vote campaign, majority voting structures can serve to enhance dialogue between shareholders and managers.[148] From this perspective, that shareholders rarely challenge manager selections may reflect greater compromise prior to such selections. Evidence also suggests that shareholders do exercise their authority during times of perceived crisis. Certainly the fact that shareholders were able to oust a key German CEO exemplifies this point. Additionally, shareholders in the United Kingdom have been known to cast a high percentage of dissenting votes for some directors.[149] In some cases, the dissent vote reached in excess of thirty percent, which one analyst characterized as "striking."[150] In other cases, even when shareholders' votes fall short of the majority needed to oust a director, such votes lead to the removal of directors.[151] A similar phenomenon occurred in the case of Disney, where even though shareholders' "no" votes fell short of a majority, shareholders' expression of dissent eventually prompted corporate action. In this regard, the bare statistics on shareholder voting patterns may understate the influence of shareholder voting. Here too, the fact that shareholders exercise their power of removal or dissent only in rare circumstances may reflect an optimal use of shareholder power. As Professor Bebchuk notes, the purpose of enhanced shareholder power is not to supplant managerial authority, but rather to ensure greater dialogue between shareholders and managers while ensuring that shareholders can exercise their voice under critical circumstances.[152] In this regard, the evidence may indicate that shareholders use their authority where appropriate.

B. Shareholder Democracy and Corporate Value

Professor Bainbridge and others also contend that shareholder democracy and activism will not improve firm value. In fact, U.S. studies assessing the impact of shareholder democracy and activism on firm value have yielded mixed results. At least some studies suggest that shareholder activism may have a positive impact on corporate governance structures.[153] Other studies indicate that shareholder activism has little to no link to share value and earnings.[154] Still other studies confirm the notion that shareholder activism has had a minimal impact on corporate performance.[155] These findings suggest that shareholder agitation and increased participation do not necessarily translate into greater value for shareholders.

Interestingly, a recent study in the United Kingdom supported by the London Business School contradicts such an assessment.[156] The study found a high correlation between enhanced firm value and shareholder activism on the part of institutional investors.[157] Authors of the study cautioned that the results may not have broad application to other countries, particularly the United States.[158] This is because the governance mechanisms in the United Kingdom are distinct from and in many ways more expansive than those in the United States. Thus, scholars note that legal obstacles, including the restricted shareholder nomination and director election process, impede the activism of American investors.[159] Moreover, scholars pinpoint the lack of majority vote system in the United States as hampering the ability of shareholder activism to have a positive influence on shareholder value and returns.[160] Thus, as several American scholars have noted, the governance conditions in the United Kingdom may make that country a more favorable environment for activism, increasing the likelihood that such activism will have a positive impact on shareholder returns.[161]

At the very least, the study suggests that shareholder activism can have favorable repercussions for shareholders under the right circumstances. Many of the problems associated with the U.S. governance system that have made it less ideal for effective shareholder activism, such as the majority vote system and shareholder proxy access, are now being addressed in some fashion. Thus, to the extent that American shareholders have begun to dismantle these systems, the U.K. study raises the possibility that the altered U.S. corporate governance structure—like its U.K. counterpart—may present a more favorable environment for activism. As a result, the study also raises the possibility that shareholder democracy can have a positive impact on share value and earnings.

C. Shareholder Democracy and Corporate Affairs

Some have maintained that increasing shareholder power may have little impact on corporate affairs. In fact, previous studies suggest that increasing shareholder power may not lead to greater accountability or otherwise rectify corporate governance failures. In other contexts, scholars have pointed out that shareholder activism through the shareholder proposal process represents an ineffective mechanism for altering corporate practices, particularly practices involving executive compensation schemes.[162] Thus, it is not clear that increasing shareholder power will prove effective.

At first, experiences in other countries appear to confirm the notion that increased shareholder power will do little to prevent corporate misconduct. Indeed, shareholders in other countries not only operate under a majority vote regime, but also have an expanded ability to remove directors from office.[163] This ability did not have an appreciable impact on preventing corporate misconduct. Instead, similar to the United States, those countries experienced several instances of corporate mismanagement and fraud. Proponents of majority voting have argued that a majority vote standard would increase accountability, because shareholders would have the actual ability to prevent directors from serving on the board.[164] This ability would serve as a powerful threat, and hence a powerful deterrent.[165] The fact that the majority vote regime did not appear to have such an impact in other countries, however, suggests that the threat of removal in a majority vote regime does not quell director misconduct or make directors more accountable.

Yet the United Kingdom's experience with executive compensation suggests that, in some contexts, increased shareholder power may have an impact on corporate affairs. Indeed, in 2002 the United Kingdom became the first country to require that shareholders be given an advisory vote on board pay.[166] Such a vote has apparently led to more significant dialogue between shareholders and managers on issues of compensation. Moreover, the vote apparently has had an impact on compensation levels. Thus, a recent study revealed that the compensation of top U.K. executives rose between five and six percent in 2006.[167] This increase is remarkable because for the past five years such compensation levels had increased an average of fourteen percent per year.[168] This change suggests that shareholders' enhanced authority within the corporation has had an impact on corporate affairs. In fact, many advocates of advisory votes on compensation in the United States pinpoint the United Kingdom's experience as an example of the positive impact such a vote can have on excessive compensation.[169] The fact that shareholder activism in the United Kingdom has had an impact on executive compensation is important given that the issue of compensation is one of the principle impetus for the rise in shareholder activism in the United States. From this perspective, the U.K. experience, at least with regard to compensation, supports the notion that shareholder democracy can influence corporate affairs.

To be sure, some have questioned whether the results in the UK can be replicated in the United States. Others have expressed concerns about some of the empirical data. For example, it does not appear that advisory votes on compensation have been able to better align compensation and performance at top-performing companies. In addition, advisory votes appears to have increased reliance on compensation consultants in a manner that could cause companies to generate "one size fits all" pay packages that may not be optimal. Hence, not only may the UK experience be inapplicable, but it also may reflect some negative repercussions associated with shareholder democracy.

D. Shareholder Democracy and Special Interest Governance

Several scholars have expressed concern over the possibility that granting shareholders enhanced power will give certain investors a greater ability to advance special interests at the expense of the corporation as a whole. These critics argue that the diversity of shareholders as a collective means that they will not share common interests, and thus shifting power to them would encourage rent seeking and reduce shareholder value.[170] In fact, both Professor Bainbridge and Vice Chancellor Leo Strine of the Delaware Court of Chancery question whether shareholders, if given enhanced power, will act in the best interests of the firm or will advance their own narrow self-interests.[171]

The most active shareholders of a company are often among the most susceptible to outside influences. Professor Roberta Romano points out that public pension funds face intense political pressure to focus on narrow personal and social issues.[172] Other scholars similarly pinpoint the tendency of investors such as public pensions and labor unions to pursue their own interests without regard to how they impact the corporation as a whole.[173] For example, some evidence suggests that labor unions initiate shareholder proposals after failed talks with management.[174] In this regard, many opponents contend that increasing shareholder power will only augment the ability of certain investors to advance their narrow political or personal goals.

Moreover, the type of investors on the forefront of the movement to increase shareholder power both in the United States and abroad seem to validate this concern. Specifically, in the United

States, hedge funds have been very active in the new campaign for shareholder democracy.[175] Here, too, hedge funds have played an increasingly greater role in other countries, galvanizing shareholder activism.[176] Hedge funds tend to have greater success than traditional shareholders because they have greater resources, financial innovation, and flexibility.[177] Additionally, hedge funds often couple their voting campaign with a threat of a proxy contests for corporate control.[178] This threat dramatically increases their bargaining power. Yet hedge funds often have narrow agendas that do not take into account the interests of the corporation as a whole. Hence, the presence and prominence of hedge funds in the campaign for shareholder democracy supports the notion that such democracy will not have a positive impact on the corporation as a whole.

The involvement of other investors in the new movement for shareholder democracy, however, may mitigate the problem of hedge fund activism. In the United States, institutional investors as well as pension funds also have played a major role in the new efforts to advance shareholder rights.[179] Similarly, many scholars have observed that the recent activism in other countries stems not only from hedge funds, but also from institutional investors. For instance, institutional investors in Germany have played a role in the recent wave of activism there.[180] Such investors have been focused on improving corporate governance. Thus, much of their activism has revolved around governance matters that impact all shareholders, such as CEO pay, dividends, and corporate governance codes.[181] From this perspective, the presence of other investors in the new push for shareholder democracy suggests that broad corporate concerns, as opposed to narrow special interests, may continue to be prominent. While this does not negate the potential for special interests governance, it does undermine the notion that increased shareholder power will inevitably lead to such governance.

Moreover, as Professor Bebchuk has suggested, investors who seek to advance their own self-interest are not likely to gain the support of other shareholders that may be necessary to capture the attention of corporate managers.[182] Such support is not likely to be forthcoming if an investor seeks to advance a narrow agenda.[183] Instead, investors will embrace issues that enhance the overall health of the corporation, or those that a broad range of shareholders otherwise find important.[184] This suggests that shareholder democracy may be able to weed out all but the most value-enhancing initiatives, undercutting shareholders' ability to advance personal agendas.

E. Shareholders vs. Stakeholders?

Another criticism of shareholder democracy has been that it will have a negative impact on the ability of corporations to focus on groups other than shareholders and issues beyond short-term profits.[185] Scholars such as Professors Margaret Blair and Lynn Stout have emphasized the importance of the board's role in mediating the interests of the many constituents within the corporation.[186] Critics contend that if shareholder activism shifts power away from the board, it will prevent the board from focusing on these other issues.[187] Moreover, it will ensure that the corporation only addresses issues associated with profit-making.[188]

It is certainly plausible that increased shareholder power will translate into less attention to the concerns of other stakeholders. As noted above, hedge funds have been on the forefront of the push for shareholder power. Hedge funds' primary objective, however, appears to be short-term financial gain, and such funds do not appear concerned with the interests of other constituents.[189] Activism in other countries also seems to run counter to stakeholder interests. In Japan, for example, much of the activism is aimed at facilitating takeovers.[190] Such takeovers can have a negative impact on stakeholders, leading to lost jobs for employees, diminished credit, and displacement of stores and plants to the detriment of customers and the broader community. Bebchuk points out that "game-ending"[191] decisions, like those involving a takeover, benefit shareholders and yet often have negative ramifications for stakeholders.[192] Shareholders motivated by such decisions are therefore likely to take actions that negatively impact other corporate constituents.

In many cases, however, the interests of shareholders and stakeholders converge. Indeed, many scholars recently have emphasized the notion that shareholders constitute a diverse group with different agendas.[193] Often these agendas dovetail with the interests of stakeholders. Thus, some shareholders invest with a view towards the long-term, which means that they have an interest in advancing concerns beyond immediate financial gain.[194] Indeed, these long-term investors encourage a focus on other constituents because they believe that such constituents are important to maintaining the overall health of the corporation.

More specifically, of course, many shareholders have investment goals that include supporting other constituents and broader social policies. In the United States, these so-called "social investors" include faith-based organizations, pension funds, and socially responsible investment funds.[195] In other countries, such as the United Kingdom, institutional investors have led the way in pressuring corporations to behave in socially acceptable ways.[196] Moreover, some shareholders are also stakeholders. Nowhere is this more evident than in countries like Germany and France, where employee stakeholders elect representatives to the board. In the United States, the most obvious example of this phenomenon is union pension funds, which are comprised of employees and hence presumably seek to advance the interests of employees.[197] The fact that some shareholders are also stakeholders undermines the proposition that shareholders will not take the interests of stakeholders into account.[198]

The empirical evidence on this recent wave of shareholder activism reveals that more traditional shareholders, such as institutional investors, are actually working with social investors. Accordingly, proxy data in the United States suggest that social proposals are drawing increased support from institutional and traditional investors, because these more traditional investors have begun to believe that focusing on particular stakeholder concerns, including employees, consumers, and the larger community, inures to the benefit of the entire corporation.[199] Data both in the United States and elsewhere reveal that social investors and traditional investors have joined forces, and it is this collaboration that is responsible for many of the successful shareholder votes.[200] Moreover, this collaboration has blurred the lines between governance and social issues: traditional investors have begun to view social issues as important to shareholder value while social investors have become increasingly concerned with traditional governance matters.[201] Here, the recent data suggest that increased shareholder power has not caused shareholders and stakeholders to be at odds. Instead, it has improved the fate of both shareholders and stakeholders. In this regard, shareholder democracy may enhance the interests of stakeholders, particularly because it may enhance the ability of social investors to collaborate with other investors to advance the concerns of all corporate constituents.

F. Proxy Access: Some Canadian Perspective

Although shareholders in the US view proxy access as pivotal to their shareholder empowerment movement, experiences with such access in Canada suggest that its utility may be vastly overstated. Indeed, although proxy access is available in Canada, shareholders waging a proxy contest do not take advantage of it. Canadian companies may be subject to different rules depending on whether they are incorporated federally or provincially. However, proxy access is generally available with respect to either form of incorporation. Importantly, under the federal Canadian Business Corporation Act (the "Canadian Act"), a corporation that solicits proxies must include shareholder proposals in the proxy statement, and such proposals may include nomination for director candidates so long as shareholders making such nominations represent 5% or more of the shares entitled to vote. Moreover, shareholders holding 5% or more of the voting stock may call a special meeting, including for the purpose of removing directors. Yet there is no indication that shareholders use the Canadian proxy access machinery when engaging in a proxy contests. Instead, those waging such contests engage in separate solicitations. This experience suggest that proxy access may have no impact on shareholder campaigns, and hence that the struggle in the US to obtain such access may have been unnecessary.

In fact, the Canadian experience suggest that proxy access is undesirable because it places soliciting shareholders at a strategic disadvantage, while failing to eliminate many of the costs associated with proxy solicitation. Indeed, apparently shareholders waging proxy fights in Canada, including U.S. shareholders, have steered clear of proxy access because it requires such shareholders to rely on a company's proxy machinery, which enables the company to control the solicitation process. Moreover, the proxy access rules places word limits a shareholders' proposal. Such limits undermine shareholders' ability to actively solicit other shareholders. As a result, shareholders have found it more advantageous to rely on their own separate proxy materials. Moreover, in light of word limits associated with proxy access, shareholders seeking to run a robust campaign must spend significant advertising and other funds, and hence there is very little cost-savings associated with relying on proxy access.

To be sure, the Canadian experience may be unique. Indeed, some have argued that Canadian companies have better developed avenues of communication and hence have less need for proxy access than US shareholders. Others insist that Canadian shareholders do not have an activist culture, and hence are more reluctant to engage in proxy contests and thus utilize proxy access. Then too, the ownership structure of Canadian companies may make proxy access less attractive. Indeed, in many such companies, a small number of shareholder own most of the company's shares. This means that such shareholders may be able to rely on communicative devices to influence corporate affairs. Moreover, it means that shareholders can engage in proxy solicitations without incurring costs by relying on exemptions to the proxy solicitation rules that allow solicitations of fifteen or fewer shareholders. These distinctions may suggest that the Canadian experience may not be applicable to the US, and hence may not be a good indicator of whether shareholders in the US will find proxy access a useful tool in their empowerment efforts.

III. Conclusion

Shareholders in the United States are becoming more active in asserting and exercising their voting rights. A similar phenomenon is occurring in other countries. By comparing the American experience with those of investors in other nations, this chapter provides an international perspective for the ongoing shareholder democracy debate in the United States.

As an initial matter, U.S. shareholders are not alone in their activism. Instead, such activism has taken root in many other countries where shareholders not only have sought to strengthen their voting power, but also have taken a more active role in overseeing corporate governance affairs.

Shareholder activism and the push for greater democracy may also have positive repercussions for shareholders. Indeed, studies in other countries reveal that shareholder activism may positively influence share value and earnings. To the extent that these results can be applied to shareholder efforts in the United States, they raise the possibility that shareholder democracy can achieve its goal of improving firm value. Other countries have experienced success in altering corporate practices through increased shareholder participation, which bodes well for shareholder engagement efforts in the United States. Finally, shareholder democracy does not have to undermine the interests of stakeholders. Instead, this chapter illuminates reasons why enhanced shareholder power may prove beneficial to all corporate constituents.

Shareholder democracy is not a panacea for all of the corporation's ills. Under the right circumstances, however, it can have a positive influence on corporate governance. Given the momentum that shareholder democracy campaigns now enjoy both in the United States and abroad, the debate about its desirability may now be of limited significance—such democracy, at least in some form, appears to be a fait accompli. If this is true, then American scholars would do well to investigate international experiences in shareholder democracy for insights on how U.S. corporations can harness the benefits of shareholder democracy, while minimizing its shortcomings.

NOTES

Chapter 2

1. *See* 17 CFR § 240.14(a).
2. *See* Lisa M. Fairfax, *Virtual Shareholder Meetings Reconsidered*, 40 Seton Hall L. Rev. 1367 (2010).
3. *See id.*
4. *See* Del. Code Ann., tit. 8, § 211 (2000).
5. *See* Fairfax, *supra* note 2 at 1366–67.
6. *See id.* at 1381.
7. *See* Shareholder Choice Regarding Proxy Materials, 72 Fed. Reg. 42,222 (Aug. 1, 2007).
8. *See* Jeffrey N. Gordon, *Proxy Contests in an Era of Increasing Shareholder Power: Forget Issuer Proxy Access and Focus on E-Proxy*, 61 Vand. L. Rev. 475, 487 (2008).
9. *See* Fabio Saccone, E-Proxy Reform, Activism, and the Decline in Retail Shareholder Voting, 4 December 2010 (Report from The Conference Board).
10. *See* TheCorporateCounsel.net Blog, http://www.thecorporate counsel.net/blog/archive/001628.html (Jan. 15, 2008 6:07 EST).
11. *See* Saccone, *supra* note 9 at 5.
12. *See SEC Announces Efforts to Educate Investors About Participating in Corporate Elections*, Feb. 22, 2010, *available* at http://www.sec.gov/news/press/2010/2010-23.htm.
13. *See New Shareholder Voting Rules for the 2010 Proxy Season*, *available at* http://www.sec.gov/investor/alerts/votingrules2010.htm.
14. *See id.*
15. See *Roundtable on Proxy Voting Mechanics, Topic One: Share Ownership and Voting*, *available at* http://www.sec.gov/spotlight/proxyprocess/proxyvotingbrief.htm.
16. *See Order Approving Proposed Rule Change*, July 1, 2009, *available at* http://www.sec.gov/rules/sro/nyse/2009/34-60215.pdf.

17. *See* Report and Recommendations of the Proxy Working Group to the New York Stock Exchange 11 (2006), *available at* http://www.nyse.com/pdfs/PWG_REPORT.pdf.

18. *See* Iman Anabtawi and Lynn Stout, *Fiduciary Duties for Activist Shareholders*, 60 Stan. L. Rev. 1255, 1307 (2008).

Chapter 3

1. *See* Blasius Indus., Inc. v. Atlas Corp., 564 A.2d 651, 659 (Del Ch. 1988).

2. *See* Anat R. Admati and Paul Pfleiderer, *The "Wall Street Walk" and Shareholder Activism: Exit as a Form of Voice*, Oct. 2005, *available at* http://papers.ssrn.com/sol3/papers.cfm?abstract_id=1015940.

3. *See* Henry R. Horsey, *The Duty of Care Component of the Delaware Business Judgment Rule*, 19 Del. J. Corp. L. 971, 982 (1994) (discussion reported cases with liability findings associated with breaches of the duty of care); Stuart Cohn, *Demise of the Director's Duty of Care: Judicial Avoidance of Standards and Sanctions Through the Business Judgment Rule*, 62 Tex. L. Rev. 591, 593–594 (1983) (finding seven reported cases imposing legal liability); Joseph Bishop, *Sitting Ducks & Decoys: New Trends in the Indemnification of Corporate Directors and Officers*, 77 Yale L. J. 1078, 1099 (1968) (finding four such cases).

4. *See* Bernard Black, et al., Outside Director Liability, 58 Stan. L. Rev. 1055 (2006).

5. *See id.*

6. *See* John Coffee, *Regulating the Market for Corporate Control: A Critical Assessment of the Tender Offer's Role in Corporate Governance*, 84 Colum. L. Rev. 1145, 1216 (1984).

7. *See id.* at 1215.

8. *See id.* at 1204; James D. Cox, *Compensation, Deterrence and the Market as Boundaries for Derivative Suit Procedures*, 52 Geo. Wash. L. Rev. 745, 753 (1984).

9. *See* Lucian Bebchuk, *The Case for Increasing Shareholder Power*, 118 Harv. L. Rev. 833 (2005).

10. *See* Stephen Bainbridge, *Director Primacy and Shareholder Disempowerment*, 119 Harv. L. Rev. 1735, 1746 (2005) [hereinafter Bainbridge, *Director Primacy*]; Stephen Bainbridge, *The Case for Limited Shareholder Voting Rights*, 53 UCLA L. Rev. 601, 624 (2006) [hereinafter Bainbridge, *Shareholder Voting Rights*]; William Bratton and Michael Wachter, *The Case Against Shareholder Empowerment*, 158 U. Pa. L. Rev. 653 (2010).

11. *No Democracy Please, We're Shareholders,* The Economists, April 29, 2004, *available at* http://www.law.harvard.edu/faculty/bebchuk/the-economist-4-29.htm.

12. *See* Bebchuk, *supra* note 9 at 837.

13. *See* Alon Brav, Wei Jiang, Frank Partnoy and Randall Thomas, *Hedge Fund Activism, Corporate Governance, and Firm Performance,* 63 J. of Finance 1729 (2008).

14. *See* Iman Anabtawi, *Some Skepticism About Increasing Shareholder Power,* 53 UCLA L. Rev. 561, 577 (2006) (noting potential for increased rent-seeking behavior).

15. *See* Margaret M. Blair & Lynn A. Stout, *A Team Production Theory of Corporate Law,* 85 VA. L. Rev. 247, 304–05 (1999).

16. *See id.*

17. *See* Bainbridge, *Director Primacy, supra* note 10 at 1746; Bainbridge, *Shareholder Voting Rights, supra* note 10 at 624.

18. *See* Lynn Stout, *The Shareholder as Ulysses: Some Empirical Evidence on Why Investors in Public Corporations Tolerate Board Governance,* 152 U. Pa. L. Rev. 667, 671 (2003).

19. Roberta Romano, *Less is More: Making Institutional Investor Activism a Valuable Mechanism of Corporate Governance,* 18 Yale J. on Reg. 174, 182 (2001).

20. *See* John Karpoff, *The Impact of Shareholder Activism on Target Companies: A Survey of the Empirical Findings,* Sept. 10, 2001, *available at* http://faculty.london.edu/dgromb/papers/Karpoff(WP2001).pdf; Stuart L. Gillian, Laura t. Starks, *Corporate Governance Proposals and Shareholder Activism: The Role of Institutional Investors,* 57 J. of Fin. Econ. 275, 300 (2000).

21. *See* Lisa M. Fairfax, *Making the Corporation Safe for Shareholder Democracy,* 69 Ohio State L.J. 53 (2008).

Chapter 4

1. *See* Bd. Of Governors of the Fed. Reserve Sys., *Flow of Funds Accounts of the United States: Annual Flows and Outstandings 1945–1954,* at 83, *available at* http://www.federalreserve.gov/releases/z1/Current/annuals/a1945-1954.pdf [hereinafter Flow of Funds 1945–1954]. Statistics for individual investors stem from the category of households and nonprofits, a category that includes retail investors as well as individuals who hold large blocks of shares. Some sources suggest that individuals directly owned more than 93% of U.S. equities in 1950. *See* Carolyn Brancato and Stephen Rabimov, The 2008 Institutional Investment Report: Trends in Institutional Investor Assets and Equity Ownership of U.S. Corpo-

RATIONS 20 (Table 10) (Sept. 2008) (indicating that institutional investors accounted for approximately 6.1% of equity holders in 1950).

2. *See* Bd. Of Governors of the Fed. Reserve Sys., *Flow of Funds Accounts of the United States: annual Flows and Outstandings* 1965–1974, at 83, *available at* http://www.federalreserve.gov/releases/z1/Current/annuals/a1965-1974.pdf [hereinafter Flow of Funds 1965–1974].

3. *See* Bd. Of Governors of the Fed. Reserve Sys., *Flow of Funds Accounts of the United States: annual Flows and Outstandings* 1985–1994, at 83, *available at* http://www.federalreserve.gov/releases/z1/Current/annuals/a1985-1994.pdf [hereinafter Flow of Funds 1985–1994].

4. *See* Bd. Of Governors of the Fed. Reserve Sys., *Flow of Funds Accounts of the United States: annual Flows and Outstandings* 2005–2009, at 83, *available at* http://www.federalreserve.gov/releases/z1/Current/annuals/a2005-2009.pdf [hereinafter Flow of Funds 2005–2009].

5. *See* Brancato and Rabimov, *supra* note 1 at 20; Flow of Funds 1945–1950, *supra* note 1 at 83.

6. *See Flow of Funds* 1965–1974, *supra* note 2 at 83.

7. *See Flow of Funds* 1985–1994, *supra* note 3 at 83.

8. *See Flow of Funds* 2005–2009, *supra* note 4 at 83.

9. *See* The Conference Board, *U.S. Institutional Investors Boost Ownership of U.S. Corporations to New High*, Sept. 2, 2008, *available at* http://www.conference-board.org/utilities/pressdetail.cfm?press_id=3466.

10. *See* Marcel Kahan and Edward Rock, *Embattled CEOs*, 88 Tex. L. Rev. 987, 997 n. 26 (2010).

11. *See Flow of Funds* 2005–2009, *supra* note 4 at 95 n. 1 (indicating that the asset totals relating to household and nonprofit organizations include domestic hedge funds).

12. *See* Matteo Tonello and Stehan Rabimov, THE 2010 INSTITUTIONAL INVESTMENT REPORT: TRENDS IN ASSET ALLOCATION AND PORTFOLIO COMPOSITION, 27 (Table 13).

13. *See id.*

14. *See id.*

15. *See id.* at 29 (Table 16).

16. *See id.*

17. *See id.* at 11 (Table 3).

18. *See id.*

19. *See id.* at 50.

20. *See id.* at 51 (Chart 22).

21. *See id.* at 53 (Table 21).

22. *See id.* at 11 (Table 3).

23. *See id.*

24. *See* Stephen J. Choi and Jill Fisch, *On Beyond Calpers: Survey Evidence on the Developing Role of Public Pension Funds in Corporate Governance*, 61 Van. L. Red. 315, 317 (2008).

25. *See id.* at 326–328.

26. *See id.*

27. *See id.*

28. *See* Roberta Romano, *Public Pension Fund Activism in Corporate Governance Reconsidered*, 93 Colum. L. Rev. 795 (1993).

29. *See* Stewart J. Schwab and Randall S. Thomas, *Realigning Corporate Governance: Shareholder Activism by Labor Unions*, 96 Mich. L. Rev. 1018, 1023 (1998); Ashwini Agrawal, *Corporate Governance Objectives of Labor Union Shareholders: Evidence from Proxy Voting*, 2008, *available at* http://archive.nyu.edu/bitstream/2451/27848/2/wpa08006.pdf.

30. *See* Agrawal, *supra* note 29.

31. *See* Schwab and Thomas, *supra* note 29 at 1023.

32. *See Facts about the AFL-CIO's Proxy Votes, available at* http://www.afl cio.org/corporatewatch/capital/upload/facts_aflcio_proxy_votes.pdf.

33. *See* Kahan and Rock, *supra* note 10 at 1001–04.

34. *See* Marcel Kahan and Edward Rock, *Hedge Funds in Corporate Governance and Corporate Control*, 155 U. Pa. L. Rev. 1021, 1046 (2007).

35. *See* Alon Brav, Wei Jiang, Frank Partnoy and Randall Thomas, *Hedge Fund Activism, Corporate Governance, and Firm Performance*, 63 J. of Finance 1729, 1734 (2008) (citing studies).

36. *See id.*

37. *See id.*

38. See CSX Corporation v. The Children's Investment Fund, 562 F.Supp 2d 511 (SDNY 2008).

39. *See* Stephen Choi, et al., *Director Elections and The Role of Proxy Advisors*, 82 S.Cal. L. Rev. 649, 652–660 (2009); *Concept Release on the U.S. Proxy System*, 106, Rel. No. 34-62495, *available at* http://www.sec.gov/rules/concept/2010/34-62495.pdf.

40. *See* 17 C.F.R. § 270.206(4)-6 (2003) and 17 C.F.R. § 270.30b1-4.

41. *See* Chris Kentouris, *Proxy Advisory Firms: To Regulate or Not?*, Securities Technology Monitor, Dec. 10, 2010, *available at* http://www.securitiestechnologymonitor.com/news/proxy-advisory-heat-26538-1.html?zkPr intable=true.

42. *See* Concept Release, *supra* note 38 at 116.

43. *See* Choi, *supra* note 38 at 696.

44. *See id.*

45. *See* Stephen Choi, et al., *The Power of Proxy Advisors: Myth or Reality*, 59 Emory L. J. 870, 905–906 (2010).

46. *See id.* at 871 (discussing commentators' views on proxy advisors' influence).

Chapter 5

1. *See* 17 CFR § 240.14a-8 (a).
2. *See* Exchange Act Release No. 378 (Sept. 24, 1935).
3. *See* Exchange Act Release No. 12,599, n 16 (July 7, 1976) (citing Hearings Before the House Comm. On Interstate and Foreign Commerce on H.R. 1493).
4. *See* Exchange Act Release No. 3347 (Dec. 18, 1942).
5. *See* Exchange Act Release No. 12,999 (Nov. 22, 1976).
6. *See* Exchange Act Release No. 34-40018 (May 21, 1998).
7. *See* 17 CFR § 240.14a-8(b).
8. *See* Exchange Act Release No. 20, 091 (Aug. 16, 1983).
9. *See* 17 CFR § 240.14a-8(c).
10. *See* 17 CFR § 240.14a-8(d).
11. *See* 17 CFR § 240.14a-8(e).
12. *See* 17 CFR § 240.14a-8(h).
13. *See* 17 CFR § 240.14a-8(f).
14. *See* Division of Corporation Finance, *Shareholder Proposal No-Action Letters Issued Under Exchange Act Rule 14a-8*, *available at* http://www.sec.gov/divisions/corpfin/cf-noaction/14a-8.shtml.
15. *See* Del. Conts. § 118 (2007).
16. *See* SEC, *Certification of Questions of Law Arising from Rule 14a-8 Proposal by Shareholder of CA, Inc.*, *available at* http://www.sec.gov/rules/other/2008/ca14a8cert.pdf.
17. *See* CA, Inc. v. AFSCME Employees Pension Plan, 953 A.2d 227 (Del. 2008).
18. *See* Division of Corporate Finance: Staff Legal Bulletin No. 14A, *Shareholder Proposals*, (July 12, 2002), *available at* http://www.sec.gov/interps/legal/cfslb14a.htm.
19. *See* Shareholder Proposals, Exchange Act Release No. 56, 160, 72 Fed. Reg. 43, 466, 43,478 (proposed July 27, 2007).
20. *See id.* at 43,469.
21. *See* Shareholder Proposal Relating to the Election of Directors, Exchange Act Release No. 56, 161, 72 Fed. Reg. 43, 488 (proposed July 27, 2007).
22. *See* RiskMetrics Group, *2009 Proxy Season Scorecard* (as of Dec. 12, 2009), *available at* http://www.riskmetrics.com/knowledge/proxy_season_watchlist_2009.
23. *See* 2009 RISKMETRICS GROUP POSTSEASON REPORT: A NEW VOICE IN GOVERNANCE: GLOBAL POLICYMAKERS SHAPE THE ROAD TO REFORM 5 (October 2009) [hereinafter 2009 Proxy Report].
24. *See id.*; *Treasury Announces New Restrictions on Executive Compensation*, Feb. 4, 2009, *available at* http://www.ustreas.gov/press/releases/tg15.htm.

25. *See* Dodd-Frank Wall Street Reform and Consumer Protection Act, Pub. L. 111-203, H.R. 4173, §§ 951 and 971 (2010), *available at* http://docs.house.gov/rules/finserv/111_hr4173_finsrvcr.pdf [hereinafter Dodd-Frank Act].

26. *See id.* at § 951(a)(1).

27. *See* Fabrizio Ferri & David Maber, *Say on Pay Votes and CEO Compensation: Evidence from the UK*, 20, *available at* http://papers.ssrn.com/sol3/papers.cfm?abstract_id=1420394.

28. *See* Jeffrey N. Gordon, *"Say on Pay": Cautionary Notes on the U.K. Experience and the Case for Shareholder Opt-in*, 46 Harv. J. on Legis. 323, 352–353 (2009); Andrew Lund, *Say on Pay's Bundling Problems*, 12–13 (2010), *available at* http://ssrn.com/abstract=1598384.

29. *See 2009 Proxy Season Report, supra* note 23.

30. *See id.* at 5.

31. *See* Lucian Bebchuk, *The Case for Increasing Shareholder Power*, 118 Harv. L. Rev. 833, 854 (2005).

32. *See id.* at 5.

33. *See id.*

34. *See id.*

35. *See id.* at 9.

36. *See* Lisa M. Fairfax, *Making the Corporation Safe for Shareholder Democracy*, 69 Ohio State L. J 53, 79–96 (2008).

37. *See 2009 Proxy Report, supra* note 23 at 15.

38. *See id.*

39. *See id.*

40. *See id.* at 16.

41. *See* Joao Dos Santos and Chen Song, ANALYSIS OF THE WEALTH EFFECTS OF SHAREHOLDER PROPOSALS, 3–4, July 22, 2008, *available at* http://www.uschamber.com/sites/default/files/reports/080722wfi_shareholder.pdf (Study Commissioned by the US Chamber of Commerce).

42. *See id.* at 12.

Chapter 6

1. *See* William K. Sjostrom and Young Sang Kim, *Majority Voting for the Election of Directors*, 40 Conn. L. Re. 459, 472 (2007); Comm. on Corporate Laws of the Section of Bus. Law, PRELIMINARY REPORT OF THE COMM. ON CORPORATE LAWS ON VOTING BY SHAREHOLDERS FOR THE ELECTION OF DIRECTORS 9 (2006), *available at* http://www.abanet.org/buslaw/committees/CL270000pub/directorvoting/20060117000001.pdf.

2. *See* Claudia H. Allen, STUDY OF MAJORITY VOTING IN DIRECTOR ELECTIONS, at 10–11 n. 9 (lasted updated Nov. 20, 2007), *available at*

http://www.ngelaw.com/files/upload/majoritystudy111207.pdf. (revealing a "relatively limited" number of corporations with majority voting regimes before to the majority vote campaign began).

3. *See* Securities Exchange Act of 1934 Rule 14a-4(b)(2), 17 C.F.R. § 240.14a-4(b)(2) (2007).

4. *See id.*

5. *See* Securities Exchange Act of 1934 Rule 14a-1(1), 17 C.F.R. § 240.14a-1(1) (2007). *See also* Jeffrey D. Bauman, et al., CORPORATIONS: LAW AND POLICY 528–29 (6th ed. 2007) (discussing amendments and their impact); Iman Anabtawi and Lynn Stout, *Fiduciary Duties for Activist Shareholders*, 60 Stan. L. Rev. 1255, 1276–77 (2008) (same).

6. *See* Riskmetrics Group, Inc., 2009 Postseason Report, A NEW VOICE IN GOVERNANCE: GLOBAL POLICYMAKERS SHAPE THE ROAD TO REFORM, Oct. 2009, at 10, *available at* http://www.riskmetrics.com//system/files/private/2009_PSR_Public_final.pdf [hereinafter *2009 Postseason Report*].

7. *See id.* at 4, 10. In 2008, only 32 directors failed to receive majority support. According to Riskmetrics Group, shareholders' lack of support stemmed from compensation practices at the firms in the S&P 500, and the adoption of poison pills without shareholder approval at smaller firms. *See id.*

8. In connection with the financial crisis, shareholders used vote withholding to signal their dissatisfaction with directors at financial firms where shareholders believed executive compensation packages were inconsistent with company performance. Thus, investors withheld significant percentage of their vote from compensation committee members of at least three firms where there was significant concern about the pay packages such members had oversaw. *See id.* at 6–7. For example, investors at Citigroup withheld more than twenty five percent of their votes from members of the compensation committee who they believed were responsible for the CEO's departure compensation. *See id.* at 6–7. Along these same lines, investors withheld more than twenty-five percent of their votes from nine directors at Washington Mutual amidst concerns about its bonus policies. RM at 9.

9. *See* Joseph Grundfest, *Just Vote No: A Minimalist Strategy for Dealing with Barbarians Inside the Gates*, 45 Stan. L. Rev. 857, 908 (1993).

10. *See id.*

11. Diane Del Guercio, Laura Seery & Tracie Woidtke, *Do Boards Pay Attention When Institutional Investor Activists "Just Vote No"?*, 90 J. FIN. ECON. 84, 85 (2008). The study found that, with respect to campaigns motivated by firm performance and strategy, "boards take a variety of value-enhancing actions: 31% of these targets experience disciplinary CEO turnover and 50% of the remaining targets that do not dismiss the CEO make other strategic changes." *Id.* at 86.

12. *See In re* Walt Disney Co. Derivative Litig., 731 A 2d 342, 352 (Del. Ch. 1998).

13. *See id.*

14. *See In re* Walt Disney Co. Derivative Litig., 906 A2d 27, 41–43 (Del. 2006); *See In re Walt Disney*, 731 A2d at 350–52.

15. *See In re Walt Disney*, 731 A2d at 352.

16. *See In re Walt Disney*, 906 A2d at 35. The Delaware Chancery Court originally estimated the severance package to be approximately $140 million. *See In re Walt Disney*, 731 A.2d at 350.

17. *See* Lori B. Marino, *Executive Compensation and the Misplaced Emphasis on Increasing Shareholder Access to the Proxy*, 147 U. PA. L. REV. 1205, 1216 (1999) (noting estimates of Ovitz's severance package between $15 million and $90 million). Others indicated that Disney executives originally believed Ovitz's exit package would be as low as $30 million. *See* Kim Masters, *Ovitz and Out at Disney*, Time, Dec. 23, 1996, *available at* http://www.time.com/time/magazine/article/0,9171,985730,00.html.

18. *See In re Walt Disney*, 906 A2d at 35 and 35 n.1 (describing litigation); *In re Walt Disney*, 731 A2d at 342 (describing litigation); Brehm v. Eisner, 746 A.2d 244 (Del. 2000).

19. *See In re Walt Disney*, 906 A.2d at 56.

20. Initial totals indicated that shareholders had withheld only 42% of their vote against Eisner. Institutional S'holder Servs., 2004 POSTSEASON REPORT: A NEW CORPORATE GOVERNANCE WORLD: FROM CONFRONTATION TO CONSTRUCTIVE DIALOGUE 5 (2004). Disney shareholders first used the vote no campaign to express their outrage right after Ovitz's termination, withholding 13% of their vote against five Disney directors in the 1997 election cycle. *See* Marino, *supra* note 17 at 1216; Stewart J.Schwab & Randall S. Thomas, *Realigning Corporate Governance: Shareholder Activism by Labor Unions*, 96 MICH. L. REV. 1018, 1073 (1998).

21. *See* Allen, *supra* note 2 at v.

22. *See id.; see also* 2006 Post Season Report: Spotlight on Executive Pay and Board Accountability 16 (2006) [hereinafter *2006 Proxy Season Report*].

23. *See* Allen, *supra* note 2 at v; *2006 Proxy Season Report, supra* note 22 at 16.

24. *See* Allen, *supra* note 2 at v; *2006 Proxy Season Report, supra* note 22 at 16.

25. *See 2006 Proxy Season Report, supra* note 22 at 16.

26. *See* John Olson, et al., *Excerpts from Recent Developments in U.S. Securities and Corporate Finance*, 1820 PLI/Corp 105, 159 (2010).

27. See Riskmetrics Group, 2008 Postseason Report 4 (2008), *available at* http://www.riskmetrics.com/white_papers [hereinafter *2008 Proxy Season Report*].

28. *See* O'Melveny & Myers, LLP, 2010 Proxy Season Guide 3, *available at* http://www.omm.com/files/upload/OMelvenyMyers-2010-Proxy-Guide.pdf [hereinafter OMM Proxy Guide]. According to Riskmetrics, from January to June 30 of 2009, the average level of shareholder support for such proposals was 56%. *See 2009 Postseason Report, supra* note 6 at 5.

29. *See* Allen, *supra* note 2 at 10–11 n.9. Allen discovered 107 companies with a majority vote rule in place prior to the majority vote movement which began during the 2005 proxy season. Another study found only thirty company with a majority vote regime prior to 2005. *See* Brooke Masters, *Proxy Measures Pushing Corporate Accountability Gain Support*, Wash. Post, June 17, 2006, at A1.

30. *See 2008 Postseason Report, supra* note 27 at 33.

31. *See* Olson, *supra* note 26 at 159.

32. Professor Julian Velasco points out that true majority voting represents a system whereby a director must receive an affirmative vote of the majority of the outstanding votes entitled to vote at the director election, while simple majority voting requires that a director receive the affirmative vote of a majority of the shares present at the meeting. Majority voting relates to a system whereby a director need only receive a majority of the votes cast in her favor, without regard to votes abstained. *See* Julian Velasco, *Taking Shareholder Rights Seriously*, 41 UC Davis L. Rev. 605, 652–653 (2007). Hence, a true majority voting rule represents the most difficult system under which a director seeks to be elected, while the difference between simple majority voting and majority voting is that the former takes abstained votes into consideration. This chapter uses the term "true majority voting" to refer to each of these systems requiring directors to receive a majority of the shareholder vote.

33. *See* Kim and Sjostrom, *supra* note 1 at 480.

34. *See* National Association of Corporate Directors, Directorship, *Majority Voting for Director Elections*, Dec. 16, 2008, *available at* http://www.directorship.com/majority-voting-for-director-elections/.

35. *See* Olson, *supra* note 26 at 159.

36. *See, e.g.*, Del. Code Ann. tit. 8, § 216(3) (Supp. 2008); Model Bus. Corp. Act § 7.28(a) (2007); Allen, *supra* note 2, at 10–11 n.9.

37. *See* Allen, *supra* note 2 at v–vi.

38. *See* Model Bus. Corp. Act § 10.22(a)(2) (2007); Comm. on Corporate Laws, *Changes in the Model Business Corporation Act—Amendments to Chapter 7 and Related Provisions Relating to Shareholder Action Without a Meeting, Chapters 8 and 10 Relating to Shareholder Voting for the Election of Directors, and Chapter 13 Relating to Appraisal and Other Remedies for Fundamental Transactions*, 61 Bus. Law. 1427, 1432–33 (2006).

39. *See* Del. Code Ann., tit. 8, § 216 (Supp. 2008).

40. *See* Del. Code. Ann., tit. 8, § 141(b) (Supp. 2008).

41. *See* ALLEN, *supra* note 2, at vi (pinpointing amendments to corporate codes by Maine, Texas, Utah, and Virginia). Apparently Oklahoma has pending legislation also covering contingent and irrevocable director resignations. *See* Olson, *supra* note 26 at 160.

42. *See* Ted Allen, *Reform Bill Won't Include Majority Voting Mandate*, June 24, 2010, *available at* http://blog.riskmetrics.com/gov/2010/06/house-agrees-to-drop-majority-voting-mandate.html.

43. *See* REPORT AND RECOMMENDATIONS OF THE PROXY WORKING GROUP TO THE NEW YORK STOCK EXCHANGE, June 5, 2006, 14, *available at* http://www.nyse.com/pdfs/PWG_REPORT.pdf [hereinafter Proxy Working Group Report].

44. *See* NYSE, Inc., Rule 452 (2009), *available at* http://rules.nyse.com/nysetools/Exchangeviewer.asp?SelectedNode=chp_1_2&manual=/nyse/nyse_rules/nyse-rules.

45. *See Proxy Working Grou Reportp, supra* note 43 at 9.

46. *See* SEC Release No. 34-60215, *available at* http://sec.gov/rules/sro/nyse/2009/34-60215.pdf.

47. *See* Dodd-Frank Wall Street Reform and Consumer Protection Act, Pub. L. 111-203, H.R. 4173, § 957 (2010) [hereinafter Dodd-Frank Act].

48. *See* Sjostrom and Kim, *supra* note 1 at 463.

49. *See* DEL. CODE ANN., tit. 8 § 141(b) (Supp. 2008); MODEL BUS. CORP. ACT § 8.05(e) (2009).

50. *See* Allen, *supra* note 2 at vi (noting that 61% of companies that have adopted some form of majority voting are incorporate in Delaware).

51. *See* NACD Directorship, Majority Voting for Director Elections, Dec. 16, 2008, *available at* http://www.directorship.com/majority-voting-for-director-elections (citing study by the Corporate Library).

52. *See* Olson, *supra* note 26 at 160.

53. *See* Latham & Watkins LLP, *Majority Voting for Directors Revisited*, January 25, 2006, at 4, *available at* http://www.lw.com/upload/pubContent/_pdf/pub1472_1.pdf.

Chapter 7

1. *See* Facilitating Shareholder Director Nominations, Exchange Act Release No. 34-62764, at 315 (Aug. 25, 2010), *available at* http://www.sec.gov/rules/final/2010/33-9136.pdf.

2. *See* Marc Weingarten, et al., *Reimbursement of Proxy Contest Expenses for Incumbents and Insurgents*, Activist Investing Developments, Fall 2007, at 1, *available at* http://www.srz.com/files/News/f98802f1-dfdf-4208-9e40-c28159cf1c45/Presentation/NewsAttachment/e917ee9b-de05-

4ed1-a0d7-6b0eaf350b47/filesfilesArticle%20-%20AI%20-%20fall06%20-%20Reimbursement.pdf.

3. *See* White, *War of Words Rages over Lockheed*, L.A. Times, March 28, 1990, at D1.

4. *See* An Act to Amend Title 8 of the Delaware Code Relating to the General Corporation Law, *available at* http://legis.delaware.gov/LIS/lis145.nsf/vwLegislation/HB+19/$file/legis.html?open. See 8 Del. Code § 113 (2009).

5. *See* Section 3.4 of the Amended and Restated Bylaws of Health-South Corporation filed as Exhibit 3.3 to the Quarterly Report on Form 10-Q dated November 4, 2009.

6. *See* Lucian Bebchuk, *The Myth of the Shareholder Franchise*, 93 Va. L. Rev. 675, 683 (2007); Lucian Bebchuk, *The Case for Increasing Shareholder Power*, 118 Harv. L. Rev. 833, 856 (2005).

7. *See id.*

8. *See* Charles Nathan and Dennis Craythorn, *The 2009 Proxy Season and the Year of Investor Anger*, New York Law Journal, Nov. 17, 2008, at 4, http://www.law.harvard.edu/programs/olin_center/corporate_governance/MediaMentions/11-17-08_NYLJ.pdf; In Proxy fights, Odds in Favor of Dissidents, Aug. 23, 2007, http://blogs.reuters.com/reuters-dealzone/2007/08/23/after-all-the-punches-proxy-fights-win-half-the-time/.

9. *See id.*

10. *See* John Laide, *Proxy Fight Season*, SharkRepellent.net, Feb. 4, 2010, *available at* https://www.sharkrepellent.net/request?an=dt.getPage&st=1&pg=/pub/rs_20100204.html&Proxy_Fight_Season&rnd=284029.

11. *See id.*

12. *See* Nathan and Craythorn, *supra* note 8 at 4.

13. *See id.*

14. *See id.*

15. *See* John Laide, *Proxy Fight Volume and Success Rates Decline*, June 4, 2010, *available at* https://www.sharkrepellent.net/request?an=dt.getPage&st=1&pg=/pub/rs_20100624.html&&Proxy_Fight_Volume_and_Success_Rates_Decline&rnd=906184.

16. *See* Josh Fineman, *Peltz Will Seek Heinz Seats Again if He Doesn't Win*, Bloomberg, Aug. 9, 2006, *available at* http://www.bloomberg.com/apps/news?pid=newsarchive&sid=aW_I0qZbmueU&refer=home.

17. *See Trian Group Files Preliminary Proxy Statement for Heinz; Seeks Minority Representation on Behalf of All Heinz Shareholders; Pledges to Work with Heinz Directors to Deliver Results and Improve Value,* June 22, 2006, *available at* http://www.heinz.com/our-company/press-room/press-releases/press-release.aspx?ndmConfigId=1012072&newsId=20060622005776; *Heinz Details Superior Value and Growth Plan for Fiscal Years 2007 and 2008,* June 1, 2006, *available at* http://www.heinz.com/our-company/

press-room/press-releases/press-release.aspx?ndmConfigId=1012072&news Id=20060601005422.

18. *See Heinz Directors Reject Peltz/Trian Demand for Board Representation, Based on Plan Content and Governance Record; As Previously Announced, Heinz Will Update Shareholders on its Superior Value and Growth Plan on June 1,* May 24, 2006, *available at* http://www.heinz.com/our-company/press-room/press-releases/press-release.aspx?ndmConfigId=1012072&newsId=20060524005985; *Heinz Highlights Hypocrisy of the Peltz/Trian Slate,* July 17, 2006, *available at* http://www.heinz.com/our-company/press-room/press-releases/press-release.aspx?ndmConfigId=1012072&newsId=20060717005688.

19. *See Director Voting Results Certified in Heinz Proxy Contest,* Sept. 15, 2006, *available at* http://www.heinz.com/our-company/press-room/press-releases/press-release.aspx?ndmConfigId=1012072&newsId=20060915005382.

20. *See* Shawn Tully, *The Reinvention of Nelson Peltz: The Former Takeover Titan is Now a Brand Builder—and Maybe Even the Shareholder's New Best Friend,* Fortune, Cnn.Money, March 19, 2007, *available at* http://money.cnn.com/magazines/fortune/fortune_archive/2007/04/02/8403476/index.htm.

21. *See* Rick Stouffer, *Peltz' Heinz Profit Fails to Impress Investment Experts,* Pittsburgh Tribune-Review, Feb. 8, 2010, *available at* http://www.pittsburghlive.com/x/pittsburghtrib/business/s_666152.html.

22. *See id.*

23. *See Microsoft Proposes Acquisition of Yahoo! for $31 Per Share,* Feb. 1, 2008, *available at* http://www.microsoft.com/presspass/press/2008/feb08/02-01corpnewspr.mspx.

24. *See Lawsuit Criticizes Yahoo Retention Plan,* June 3, 2008, NY-Times.com, *available at* http://dealbook.blogs.nytimes.com/2008/06/03/lawsuit-criticizes-yahoo-retention-plan/?scp=2&sq=yahoo%20employment%20retention&st=cse.

25. *See* Steve Lohr, *Microsoft and Yahoo are Linked Up. Now What?,* NY Times.com, July 29, 2009, *available at* http://www.nytimes.com/2009/07/30/technology/companies/30soft.html?scp=13&sq=yahoo+microsoft&st=nyt.

26. *See* Pershing Square Capital Management LP, Schedule 13D, filed July 5, 2007, *available at* http://sec.gov/Archives/edgar/data/27419/000090266407002284/sc13d.txt.

27. *See* Robert Berner, *Target's Credit-Card Sale: Bad Timing?,* Bloomberg Businessweek, Sept. 13, 2007, *available at,* http://www.businessweek.com/bwdaily/dnflash/content/sep2007/db20070913_987582.htm?campaign_id=rss_daily.

28. *See* Sam Black, *Ackman Lays Out Idea for Target Real Estate Spin-Off,* Minneapolis St. Paul Business Journal, Oct. 29, 2008, *available at* http://www.bizjournals.com/twincities/stories/2008/10/27/daily25.html?jst=b_l n_hl.

29. *See Target In Deal to Raise Cash*, May 6, 2008, NYTimes.com, *available at* http://www.nytimes.com/2008/05/06/business/06target.html? scp=1&sq=target+ackman&st=nyt.

30. Prior to launching the contests, Ackman did seek to obtain seats on Target's board by asking Target's nominating committee to nominate two people supported by Ackman to serve on the board. The nominating committee declined to do so.

31. *See* Jennifer Reingold, *Ackman's Target Quest Falls Flat*, Fortune Mag., May 6, 2009, *available at* http://money.cnn.com/2009/05/28/news/companies/target_ackman.fortune/index.htm?postversion=2009052818.

32. *See Proxy Advisers Split in Ackman Target Fight*, May 15, 2009, NYTimes.com, *available at* http://dealbook.blogs.nytimes.com/2009/05/19/proxy-advisers-split-in-ackman-target-fight.

33. *See id.*

34. *See* Zachery Kouwe and Joe Nocera, *Shareholders Support Target Over Ackman*, May 28, 2009, NYTimes.com, *available at* http://dealbook.nytimes.com/2009/05/28/shareholder-support-target-in-blow-to-ackman/?hpw.

35. *See Barnes & Noble Commences Mailing of Proxy Statement for 2010 Annual Meeting*, September 25, 2010, *available at* http://www.barnesandnobleinc.com/press_releases/2010_aug_25_fight_letter_wrap.html.

36. *See* Michael J. de la Merced, *Bookseller Has Setback in Struggle Over Board*, NY Times, Sept. 20, 2010, *available at* http://www.nytimes.com/2010/09/21/business/21barnes.html.

37. *See Barnes & Noble Announces Certified Results of September 28, 2010, Annual Meeting*, October 13, 2010, *available at* http://www.barnesandnobleinc.com/press_releases/2010_oct_13_certified_results.html.

Chapter 8

1. *See* Stephen Davis and Stephen Alogna, TALKING GOVERNANCE: BOARD-SHAREHOLDER COMMUNICATIONS ON EXECUTIVE COMPENSATION, 6 (Study by Millisten Center for Corporate Governance and Performance, Yale School of Management) (2008).

2. *See* Matteo Tonello and Stepehn Rabimov, THE 2010 INSTITUTIONAL INVEST REPORT: TRENDS IN ASSET ALLOCATION AND PORTFOLIO COMPOSITION 29–42 (2010).

3. *See id.*

4. *See* 17 CFR § 240.14a.

5. *See* 17 CFR § 240.14a1(2) (1992).

6. *See* Electronic Shareholder Forums, 73 Fed. Reg. 4450 (Jan. 25, 2008) (Final Rule). The rules took effect February 25, 2008.

7. *See id.* at 4453.

8. *See Shareholder Activism Wiki, Yahoo, available* at http://shareowneractivism.wikia.com/wiki/Yahoo.

9. *See Activist Investor Eric Jackson Recommends Mixed Yahoo!/Icahn Board in Upcoming Yahoo! Proxy Vote,* July 21, 2008, *available* at http://www.redorbit.com/news/general/1487663/activist_investor_eric_jackson_recommends_mixed_yahooicahn_board_in_upcoming.

10. *See* Aupreeta Das, *Update 1-Dissident Yahoo shareholder plans vote campaign,* May 4, 2008, *available* at http://www.reuters.com/article/2008/05/04/yahoo-shareholder-idUSN0434200420080504.

11. *See* RiskMetrics Group, 2007 Postseason Report: A Closer Look at Accountability and Engagement 11 (2007).

12. *See* Nora Ganim Barnes and Eric Mattson, The Fortune 500 and Blogging: Slow and Steady and Farther Along than Expected, at 3, 2008, *available* at http://www1.umassd.edu/cmr/studiesresearch/fortune500.pdf.

13. *See id.* at 4.

14. *See id.*

15. *See* Julie Jones and Cynthia McMakin, *Is Your Company Tweeting Towards Trouble?— Twitter and Securities Law Compliance,* 23 Insights 19, 20 (September 29).

16. *See* 17 CFR 240.10b-5 (2010).

17. *See* Jones and McMakin, *supra* note 15 at 21.

18. *See* 17 CFR 240, 243, 249.

19. *See* Davis and Alogna, *supra* note 1.

20. *See Compliance and Disclosure Interpretations, Regulation FD,* June 4, 2010, *available* at http://www.sec.gov/divisions/corpfin/guidance/regfd-interp.htm.

21. *See Request for Investor Dialogue: Fifth Analyst Call on Corporate Governance and Proxy Statement,* Dec. 1, 2010, *available at* http://www.shareholderforum.com/e-mtg/Library/20101201_FifthAnalyst.pdf.

22. *See* Davis and Alogna, *supra* note 1.

Chapter 9

1. *See* Robert C. Clark, CORPORATE LAW 360 (1986); Facilitating Shareholder Director Nominations, Exchange Act Release No. 34-62764, Investment Company Release No. 29, 384, 9 and 9 n.28 (Aug. 25, 2010) [hereinafter Final Proxy Access Rule], *available at* http://www.sec.gov/rules/final/2010/33-9136.pdf.

2. *See* Securities Exchange Act of 1934 Rule 14a-4, 17 C.F.R. § 240.14a-4(a)(2) (2010) (distribution to shareholders); Securities Exchange Act of 1934 Rule 14a-6, 17 C.F.R. § 240.14a-6 (filing with the SEC).

3. *See* Securities Exchange Act of 1934 Rule 14a-3, 17 C.F.R. § 240.14a-3 (2010).

4. *See* Securities Exchange Act of 1934 Rule 14a-4, 17 C.F.R. § 240.14a-4.

5. *See* Securities Exchange Act of 1934 Rule 14a-8, 17 C.F.R. § 240.14a-8 (2010).

6. *See* Securities Exchange Act of 1934 Rule 14a-8(a)(i)(8), 17 C.F.R. § 240.14a-8(i)(8).

7. *See* Security Holder Director Nominations, Exchange Act Release No. 48,626, Investment Company Act Release No. 26,206, 68 Fed. Reg. 60,784, 60,786 (proposed Oct. 23, 2003) [hereinafter 2003 Proposed Proxy Access Rule] (noting that shareholder recommendations to the board's nominating committees rarely translate into actual nominations onto the corporate ballot).

8. *See Final Proxy Access Rule, supra* note 1 at 9–10 (noting that "most, if not all, shareholders return their proxy cards in advance of the shareholder meeting," and thus shareholder candidates nominated at the meeting do not have a "realistic prospect of being elected").

9. *See Final Proxy Access Rule, supra* note 1 at 313–320; Lucian Bebchuk, *The Myth of the Shareholder Franchise*, 93 Va. L. Rev. 675, 603 (2007).

10. *See* Bebchuk, *supra* note 9 at 683 (noting the scarcity of proxy contests).

11. *See* McQuade v. Stoneham, 189 N.E. 234, 236 (NY 1934).

12. See Karey Wutkowski, *SEC to Look Outside Ballot on Proxy Access*, Reuters, Jan. 4, 2008, http://www.reuters.com/articlePrint? articleId=USN17 41224720080104; Lisa M. Fairfax, *The Future of Shareholder Democracy*, 84 Ind. L. J. 1259, 1260 (2009).

13. *See* Proposed Rule: Security Holder Director Nominations, *available at* http://www.sec.gov/rules/proposed/34-48626.htm.

14. *See* Facilitating Shareholder Director Nominations, Exchange Act Release No. 34-60089, Investment Company Act Release No. 28765, (proposed 2009), at 7, *available at* http://www.sec.gov/rules/proposed/2009/33-9046.pdf.

15. *See Final Proxy Access Rule, supra* note 1 at 343–44.

16. *See id.* at 346–47.

17. *See* Roberta Romano, *Public Pension Fund Activism in Corporate Governance Reconsidered*, 93 Colum. L. Rev. 795, 811–12 (1993).

18. Apparently the SEC briefly considered proxy access in connection with a broader review of proxy rules in 1992, but such consideration did

not rise to the level of an actual proposal. *See* Security Holder Director Nominations, Exchange Act Release No. 48,626, Investment Company Act Release No. 26,206, 68 Fed. Reg. 60,784, 60,786 (proposed Oct. 23, 2003) [hereinafter 2003 Proxy Access Proposal].

19. *See* Securities Act Release No. 2887, Securities Exchange Act Release No. 34-3347, 7 Fed. Reg. 10, 655, 10, 656 (Dec. 18, 1942).

20. *See Securit[ies] and Exchange Commission Proxy Rules: Hearings on H.R. 1493, H.R. 1821, and H.R. 2019 Before the House Comm. on Interstate and Foreign Commerce,* 78th Cong., 1st Sess., at 157 (1943) (testimony of Chairman Ganson Purcell).

21. *See* Jayne Barnard, *Shareholder Access to the Proxy Revisited,* 40 Cath. U. L. Rev. 37, 54 (1990); Jill Fisch, *From Legitimacy to Logic: Reconstructing Proxy Regulation,* 46 Vand. L. Rev. 1129, 1163 (1993).

22. *See* Barnard, *supra* note 21 at 54; Fisch, *supra* note 21 at 1163; J.A.C. Hetherington, *When the Sleeper Wakes: Reflections on Corporate Governance and Shareholder Rights,* 8 Hofstra L. Rev. 183, 214 (1979).

23. *See* Reexamination of Rules Relating to Shareholder Communications, Shareholder Participation in the Corporate Electoral Process and Corporate Governance Generally, Exchange Act Release No. 13,482, Investment Company Act Release No. 9740, 42 Fed. Reg. 23,901, 23,903 (May 11, 1977) [hereinafter Reexamination of Shareholder Participation].

24. *See id.* at 23, 903.

25. *See* Proposed Amendments to Rule 14a-8 Under the Securities Exchange Act of 1934 Relating to Proposals by Security Holders, Exchange Act Release No. 19,135, Investment Company Act Release No. 12,734, 47 Fed. Reg. 47,420, 47, 422 (proposed Oct. 14, 1982) [hereinafter 1982 Proxy Access Proposal].

26. *See id.* at 47, 422.

27. *See* Amendments to Rule 14a-8 Under the Securities Exchange Act of 1934 Relating to Proposals by Security Holders, Exchange Act Release No. 20,091, 48 Fed. Reg. 38,218, 38,218 (Aug. 16, 1983) [hereinafter 1983 Final Rule] (Final Rule).

28. *See* Division of Corporate Finance, Securities and Exchange Commission, *Staff Report on Corporate Accountability* (Sept. 4, 1980), at A60–65.

29. *See id.* at A65. *See also 2003 Proxy Access Proposal, supra* note 18 at 60, 785.

30. *See Division of Corporate Finance, supra* note 28 at A65.

31. *See* Barnard, *supra* note 21 at 50–51.

32. *See 2003 Proposed Proxy Access Rule, supra* note 18 at 60,784.

33. *See id.* at 60,786.

34. *See id.*

35. *See id.* at 60, 794.

36. *See id.* at 60,789.

37. *See id.* at 60,789–60,790.

38. 462 F3d 121 (2d Cir. 2006).

39. *See id.* at 129.

40. In the final paragraph of the opinion, the Second Circuit noted that it was not taking sides in the policy debate regarding proxy access, particularly because "Congress has determined that such issues are appropriately the province of the SEC, not the judiciary." *See id.* at 131.

41. *See* Shareholder Proposal Relating to the Election of Directors, Exchange Act Release No. 56,161, Investment Company Act Release No. 27,914, 72 Fed. Reg. 43,488, 43,469 (proposed July 27, 2007).

42. *See id.* at 43, 488–89.

43. *See* Shareholder Proposals, Exchange Act Release No. 56,160, Investment Company Act Release No. 27,913, 72 Fed. Reg. 43,466, 43,467 (proposed July 27, 2007).

44. See id. at 43, 470.

45. Shareholder Proposals Relating to the Election of Directors, Exchange Act Release No. 56,914, Investment Company Act Release No. 28,075, 72 Fed. Reg. 70,450, 70,453 (Dec. 11, 2007) [hereinafter 2007 Final Proxy Rule].

46. *See id.* at 70, 450–451.

47. *See* Facilitating Shareholder Director Nominations, Securities Act Release No. 33-9046, Exchange Act Release No. 34-90089, Investment Company Act Release No. 28, 765, 74 Fed. Reg.29024 (June 18, 2009) [hereinafter 2009 Proposed Proxy Access Rule].

48. *See* Facilitating Shareholder Director Nominations, Exchange Act Release No. 34-62764, Investment Company Release No. 29, 384, 9 and 9 n.28 (Aug. 25, 2010) [hereinafter 2010 Final Proxy Access Rule], *available at* http://www.sec.gov/rules/final/2010/33-9136.pdf.

49. *See id.* at 23–24.

50. *See id.* at 24–25.

51. *See* Dodd-Frank Wall Street Reform and Consumer Protection Act, Pub. L. 111-203, H.R. 4173, 971(b) (2010), *available at* http://docs.house.gov/rules/finserv/111_hr4173_finsrvcr.pdf.

Chapter 10

* Other than the discussion involving proxy access in Canada, the final paragraph in the say on pay discussion, and certain formatting changes, this chapter is reprinted with permission from Lisa M. Fairfax, *Shareholder Democracy on Trial: International Perspective on the Effectiveness of Increased Shareholder Power*, 3 Va. Law & Bus. Rev. 1 (2008).

63. *See* Thaddeus C. Kopinski, Investor Pressure Leads to Election Reform, Inst'l S'holder Servs., 2006 Postseason Report 18, *available at* http://www.issproxy.com/pdf/2006PostSeasonReportFINAL.pdf [hereinafter 2006 Proxy Season Report] (noting that in the 2006 proxy season shareholders submitted more proposals seeking to institute majority voting for director elections than any other proposal).

64. *Id.; see also* Alex Kay & Gary Milner-Moore, Power to the People: The Growing Influence of Shareholder Activism, PLC Cross-Border Q., Oct.–Dec. 2006, at 40.

65. Paul Lee, Majority Voting: The Worldwide Orthodoxy, at 1, *available at* http://www.icgn.org/organisation/documents/sri/lee_document.pdf. This includes countries such as Australia, Hong Kong, India, Singapore, and South Africa.

66. *Id.; see also* Kay & Milner-Moore, *supra* note 64, at 38.

67. *See id.*

68. *See* 2006 Proxy Season Report, *supra* note 63, at 18.

69. *Id.; see also* Kay & Milner-Moore, *supra* note 64, at 38–39.

70. 2006 Proxy Season Report, *supra* note 63, at 17.

71. *See id.* This campaign is spearheaded by the Canadian Coalition for Good Governance, an organization comprised of forty-eight institutional investors that invest in the Canadian market. *See* Canadian Coalition for Good Governance, About the Canadian Coalition for Good Governance, http://www.ccgg.ca/about-the-ccgg/ (last visited Mar. 24, 2008).

72. *See* 2006 Proxy Season Report, *supra* note 63, at 17.

73. *See* Canadian Corporation for Good Governance, Guidelines, Majority Voting, http://www.ccgg.ca/guidelines/majority-voting/majority-voting-adoptees/ (last visited Mar. 24, 2008).

74. *See* 2006 Proxy Season Report, *supra* note 63, at 18.

75. *See id.*

76. *See id.*

77. *See id.*

78. *See* John Taylor, Japanese Investors Step Up Activism, Risk & Governance Blog, http://blog.issproxy.com/2006/07/000114print.html (July 7, 2006).

79. *See* Douglas G. Smith, *A Comparative Analysis of the Proxy Machinery in Germany, Japan and the United States: Implications for the Political Theory of American Corporate Finance*, 58 U. Pitt. L. Rev. 145, 171 (1995) (noting the general apathy of Japanese investors).

80. *See* Sofie Cools, The *Real Difference in Corporate Law Between the United States and Continental Europe: Distribution of Powers*, 30 Del. J. Corp. L. 697, 713 (2005); Thaddeus C. Kopinski, 2006 Preview: Continental Europe, Risk & Governance Blog, http://blog.issproxy.com/2006/02/000021print.html (Feb. 27, 2006).

81. *See id.* Under Delaware law, the board cannot block shares prior to a meeting. Instead, Delaware law only allows the board to fix a record date. *See Del. Code Ann. tit. 8, §213* (2001).

82. *See* Cools, *supra* note 80, at 713.

83. *See* Kopinski, *supra* note 80.

84. *See* Karina Litvack, Standing Up Against Share Blocking, European Pensions and Investment News, June 19, 2006, http://www.epn-magazine.com/news/fullstory.php/aid/2207/Standing_up_against_share_blocking.html.

85. *See id.*

86. *See id.* (noting activism by many investors).

87. *See id.*

88. *See* 2006 Proxy Season Report, *supra* note 63, at 40.

89. *See id.* at 38. On June 12, 2007, the E.U. Commission adopted the Directive on the Exercise of Certain Rights of Shareholders in Listed Companies. *See* Vaughn Stewart, European Commission Formally Adopts Shareholder Rights Directive, Risk & Governance Blog, http:// blog.issproxy.com/2007/06/european_commission&uscore;formally_a.htm (June 20, 2007). The directive abolishes share blocking, mandates the disclosure of voting results, and sets forth the rights of shareholders to ask questions of company officials *See id.*

90. *See* Stewart, *supra* note 89; *see also* 2006 Proxy Season Report, *supra* note 63, at 38.

91. *See* Kopinski, *supra* note 80.

92. In December 1994, the SEC approved rules proposed by the New York Stock Exchange, American Stock Exchange, and National Association of Securities Dealers that established a uniform voting standard. This new standard prohibits companies listed on the NYSE, the AMEX, or the NASDAQ system from taking any corporate action or issuing any stock that has the effect of disparately reducing or restricting the voting rights of existing common stock shareholders.

93. *But see* Shaun Martin & Frank Partnoy, *Encumbered Shares*, 2005 U. Ill. L. Rev. 775 (disagreeing with the traditional view that one share, one vote is economically optimal).

94. *See* Deminor Rating, Application of the One Share-One Vote Principle In Europe (2005), *available at* http://www.deminor.com/download.do?doc=deminorratingDocs/ABIOneShareOneVoteFullReport.pdf.

95. *See id.*

96. *See id.*

97. *See* Guido A. Ferrarini, One Share-One Vote: A European Rule? 3–4 (Univ. of Genoa and ECGI, Working Paper No. 58, 2006), *available at* http:// ssrn.com/abstract=875620.

98. *See* Martin & Partnoy, *supra* note 93.

99. *See* Ferrarini, *supra* note 97, at 2.

100. *See id.* at 5.

101. *See* Randall Thomas, *Explaining the International CEO Pay Gap: Board Capture or Market Driven?*, 57 Vand. L. Rev. 1171, 1174–76 (2004).

102. *See id.* at 1175.

103. *See* 2006 Proxy Season Report, *supra* note 63, at 14.

104. *See id.*

105. *See id.*

106. *See id.*

107. *See id.* at 15.

108. *See* Smith, *supra* note 79, at 178–79 (pinpointing significant shareholder apathy, particularly in Germany and Japan).

109. *See, e.g.,* In the Locust Position: Shareholder Activism in Japan, Economist, June 30, 2007, at 76 [hereinafter Shareholder Activism in Japan]; Smith, *supra* note 79, at 171 (noting that shareholder apathy in Japan represents a "significant barrier to shareholder participation in corporate governance").

110. *See* Smith, *supra* note 79, at 171–72.

111. *See id.*; Yoichiro Taniguchi, Japan's Company Law and the Promotion of Corporate Democracy: a Futile Attempt?, 27 Colum. J. Transnat'l L. 195, 229 (1988); Christopher Heftel, Corporate Governance in Japan: The Position of Shareholders in Publicly Held Corporations, 5 U. Haw. L. Rev. 135, 169–70 (1983).

112. *See* Smith, *supra* note 79, at 170–71.

113. *See* Shareholder Activism in Japan, *supra* note 109.

114. *See* Smith, *supra* note 79, at 172; Heftel, *supra* note 111, at 170.

115. *See* Heftel, *supra* note 111, at 107.

116. *See id.*

117. *See id.*

118. *See* Shareholder Activism in Japan, *supra* note 109.

119. *See* Taniguchi, *supra* note 111, at 228–29.

120. *See* Shareholder Activism in Japan, *supra* note 109.

121. *See id.*

122. *See id.*

123. *See id.* (explaining that traditional institutional investors in Japan have taken a more active role in Japanese governance issues alongside newer shareholder activists).

124. *See* Smith, *supra* note 79, at 186; Carter Dougherty, Deutsche Chief Looks at a Legacy of Change, Int'l Herald Trib., Dec. 16, 2005 at 13 (noting that German companies had "languished" for years without embracing shareholder activism).

125. *See* Smith, *supra* note 79, at 187.

126. *See* Dougherty, *supra* note 126; Ben McLannahan, Rebels with a Cause, CFOEurope.com, Feb. 2004, http://www.cfoeurope.com/displayStory.cfm/2383150 (describing increased shareholder democracy as a "cultural shift" among German investors).

127. *See* McLannahan, *supra* note 127.

128. *See id.*; *see also* Kay & Milner-Moore, *supra* note 64, at 44.

129. *See* Dougherty, *supra* note 126.

130. *See* Marco Becht et al., Returns to Shareholder Activism: Evidence from a Clinical Study of the Hermes U.K. Focus Fund (Eur. Corp. Governance Inst., Finance Working Paper No. 138, 2006), *available at* http://www.edebodt.net/workshop_2007/SupportFiles/ReturnToShareholderActivism.pdf; John Hendry et al., Responsive Ownership, Shareholder Value, and the New Shareholder Activism 8 (ESRC Centre for Bus. Res. Working Paper No. 297, 2004), *available at* http://www.cbr.cam.ac.uk/pdf/wp297.pdf (noting that shareholder activism has not been a widespread phenomenon in the United Kingdom).

131. *See id.* at 6.

132. *See id.*

133. *See* Becht et al., *supra* note 130, at 14–16.

134. *See id.* at 8.

135. *See id.*

136. *See id.*

142. *See* Stephen M. Bainbridge, Response, *Director Primacy and Shareholder Disempowerment*, 119 Harv. L. Rev. 1735, 1753 (2005).

143. *See* Bernard S. Black, *Shareholder Passivity Reexamined*, 89 Mich. L. Rev. 520 (1990).

144. *See* 2006 Proxy Season Report, *supra* note 63, at 18 (revealing that instances where U.K. directors receive less than majority support are rare).

145. *See, e.g.,* Cools, *supra* note 80, at 745–47; Kay & Milner-Moore, *supra* note 66, at 38–40 (explaining the French, German, and U.K. systems allowing for the removal of directors); *see also* Shareholder Activism in Japan, *supra* note 109 (noting that while corporate law is more shareholder friendly in Japan—enabling shareholders to oust the entire board without cause—Japanese shareholders tend to defer to management).

146. *See* Smith, *supra* note 79, at 170–73, 186–89 (pinpointing extralegal factors that hinder shareholder activism in Germany and Japan).

147. *Id.* at 186 (noting that shareholder apathy is "relatively great" in both Japan and Germany).

148. *See* Joseph A. Grundfest, *Just Vote No: A Minimalist Strategy for Dealing with Barbarians Inside the Gate*, 45 Stan. L. Rev. 857, 866 (1993) (noting the impact that a successful withhold-the-vote campaign may have on communication).

149. *See* Alan Brett, Manifest Info. Servs. Ltd., Voting Season Review 2002–2003 (2003), at 33–34 (presenting a study of proxy data revealing that four directors received dissenting votes in excess of thirty percent, while sixteen directors received dissents in excess of twenty percent and sixty-seven received dissents in excess of ten percent).

150. *Id.* at 34.

151. *See id.*

152. *See* Lucian Arye Bebchuk, *The Case for Increasing Shareholder Power,* 118 Harv. L. Rev. 833, 876 (2005).

153. Jonathan Karpoff, The Impact of Shareholder Value on Target Companies: A Survey of Empirical Findings 19, 26 (unpublished manuscript, 2001) *available at* http://ssrn.com/abstract=885365.

154. *See id.* at 23, 26; *see also* Bernard Black, Shareholder Activism and Corporate Governance in the U.S., in The New Palgrave Dictionary of Economics and the Law (Peter Newman ed., 1998); Stuart Gillian & Laura Starks, A Survey of Shareholder Activism: Motivation and Empirical Evidence, Contemp. Fin. Dig., Autumn 1998, at 27.

155. *See* Roberta Romano, *Less is More: Making Institutional Investor Activism a Valuable Mechanism of Corporate Governance,* 18 Yale J. on Reg. 174, 187–89 (2001).

156. *See* Becht et al., *supra* note 130, at 3, 6–7.

157. *See id.* at 6.

158. *See id.* at 3–5.

159. *See id.* at 4–5; Black, *supra* note 154, at 459; Bernard Black, *Shareholder Passivity Re-examined,* 89 Mich. L. Rev. 520 (1990).

160. *See* Becht et al., *supra* note 130, at 4–5; Cools, *supra* note 80, at 746–48.

161. *See* Becht et al., *supra* note 130, at 3–5; *see, e.g.,* Bebchuk, *supra* note 152, at 849; Bernard Black & John Coffee, *Hail Britannia?: Institutional Investor Behavior under Limited Regulation,* 92 Mich. L. Rev. 1997, 2003 (1994).

162. *See* Lori B. Morino, *Executive Compensation and the Misplaced Emphasis on Increasing Shareholder Access to the Proxy,* 147 U. Penn. L. Rev. 1205, 1236–37, 1246 (1999) (noting that executive compensation continues to rise, notwithstanding shareholders' increased ability to submit proposals related to such compensation).

163. *See* Cools, *supra* note 78, at 746.

164. *See* Brooke Masters, Proxy Measures Pushing Corporate Accountability Gain Support, Wash. Post, June 17, 2006, at A1.

165. *See id.*

166. *See* 2006 Proxy Season Report, *supra* note 63, at 14.

167. *See id.*

168. *See id.*

169. *See* H.R.1257, 110th Cong. (2007), *available at* http://www.house. gov/apps/list/speech/financialsvcs_dem/muhr1257032107.pdf.

170. *See* Iman Anabtawi, *Some Skepticism About Increasing Shareholder Power,* 53 UCLA L. Rev. 561, 575 (2006).

171. *See* Bainbridge, *supra* note 142, at 1754; Leo Strine, Jr., *Toward a True Corporate Republic: A Traditionalist Response to Bebchuk's Solution for Improving Corporate America,* 119 Harv. L. Rev. 1759, 1771 (2006).

172. *See* Roberta Romano, *Public Pension Fund Activism in Corporate Governance Reconsidered,* 93 Colum. L. Rev. 795, 811–812 (1993) (noting the distinction between public and private funds and the pressure public funds face to focus on local and social issues).

173. *See* Frank Partnoy & Randall Thomas, Gap Filling, Hedge Funds, and Financial Innovation 5, (Vanderbilt Law and Economics Research Paper No. 06-21, 2006) *available at* http://ssrn.com/abstract=931254.

174. *See id.* at 14.

175. *See* Partnoy & Thomas, *supra* note 173, at 22. For a definition of hedge funds, *see id.* at 23.

176. *See* Shareholder Activism in Japan, *supra* note 109.

177. *See* Partnoy & Thomas, *supra* note 173, at 22.

178. *See id.* at 173, at 49.

179. *See* 2006 Proxy Report, *supra* note 63, at 5, 10 (noting institutional investor and pension support for majority vote proposals).

180. *See* McLannahan, *supra* note 126.

181. *See id.*

182. *See* Partnoy & Thomas, *supra* note 173, at 14–15; Stewart Schwab & Randall S. Thomas, *Realigning Corporate Governance: Shareholder Activism by Labor Unions,* 96 Mich. L. Rev. 1018, 1035–36, 1082–83 (1998) (noting that labor initiatives cannot succeed without the support of other shareholders, which support will not emerge unless they relate to issues that have the potential to improve corporate performance); Battling for Corporate America, Economist, Mar. 11, 2006, 63 (noting that "politically motivated shareholders and hedge funds are likely to gain any real power over management only if they can persuade the usual passive majority to support them").

183. *See id.*

184. *See* Schwab & Thomas, *supra* note 184, at 1041–42.

185. *See* Bebchuk, *supra* note 152, at 912.

186. *See* Margaret M. Blair & Lynn A. Stout, *A Team Production Theory of Corporate Law,* 85 Va. L. Rev. 247, 253–54 (1999); John H. Matheson & Brent A. Olson, *Corporate Cooperation, Relationship Management, and the Trialogical Imperative for Corporate Law,* 78 Minn. L. Rev. 1443, 1446 (1994) (describing the board as a mediator for various constituent concerns).

187. *See* Blair & Stout, *supra* note 186, at 253–54, 286.

188. *See* Bebchuk, *supra* note 152, at 908; Blair & Stout, *supra* note 186, at 304–05; Lynn Stout & Iman Anabtawi, Sometimes Democracy Isn't Desirable, Wall St. J., Aug. 10, 2004 at B2 (noting that boards mediate conflicts among shareholders and other corporate constituents, and ensure that corporate policy "will not be set by an anonymous, myopic, return-hungry pack of shareholders"). *But see* Stephen Bainbridge, *Director Primacy: The Means and Ends of Corporate Governance*, 97 Nw. U. L. Rev. 547, 593–605 (2003) (advancing arguments against the conception of the board as a mediator); David Millon, *New Game Plan or Business as Usual?: A Critique of the Team Production Model of Corporate Law*, 86 Va. L. Rev. 1001, 1024–42 (2000) (stating that corporate law does not reflect the idea of the board as a mediator).

189. *See* Anabtawi, *supra* note 170, at 580; K.A.D. Camara, *Classifying Instituional Investors*, 30 J. Corp. L. 219, 239 (2005). *But see* Larry E. Ribstein, *Accountability and Responsibility in Corporate Governance*, 81 Notre Dame L. Rev. 1431, 1445 (2006) (noting that "even the most narrowly focused shareholders" are concerned about other constituents, because by advancing the concerns of such constituents, the corporation can avoid litigation and other costs associated with inflicting social harms).

190. *See* 2006 Proxy Season Report, *supra* note 63, at 43 (noting that shareholder activism has been spurred by the flurry of poison pills being introduced by Japanese firms). *See also* Shareholder Activism in Japan, *supra* note 109 (noting that much activism is focused on unwinding poison pill measures).

191. Game-ending decisions encompass decisions to merge, sell all the corporate assets, or dissolve. *See* Bebchuk, *supra* note 152, at 837.

192. *See id.* at 910.

193. *See, e.g.*, Anabtawi, *supra* note 170, at 564 (noting the various and conflicting interests among shareholders); K.A.D. Camara, *supra* note 189, at 229–42 (discussing different investors and their divergent concerns); Stout & Anabtawi, *supra* note 188 (noting that many suffer from the mistaken assumption that shareholders in public companies have a single shared interests).

194. *See* Ribstein, *supra* note 189, at 1459 ("A firm's long-run profits may depend significantly on satisfying the social demands of consumers, employees and local communities."); Anabtawi, *supra* note 170, at 579–80; Matheson & Olson, *supra* note 186, at 1487 (noting that long-term shareholders understand that a corporation's sustained growth depends on focusing on other stakeholders).

195. *See* Cynthia A. Williams & John M. Conley, *Is there an Emerging Fiduciary Duty to Consider Human Rights?*, 74 U. Cin. L. Rev. 75, 95–96 (2005); Lynn Stout, *Takeovers in the Ivory Tower: How Academics Are Learn-*

ing Martin Lipton May Be Right, 60 Bus. Law. 1435, 1449 (2005) (discussing the social shareholder).

196. While social activism is generally confined to particular investors within the United States, in other countries there appears to be a broader level of shareholder support for social issues. In fact, mainstream investors in the United Kingdom have led the way in pressuring corporations to provide more robust social-responsibility disclosures. *See* Williams & Conley, *supra* note 195, at 97–98.

197. However, it is also possible that certain pension funds will focus on issues that are not in the best interests of employees. *See* Roberta Romano, *Public Pension Fund Activism in Corporate Governance Reconsidered,* 93 Colum. L. Rev. 795, 811–14 (1993) (discussing the political pressure that often motivates the advocacy of public pension funds).

198. *See id.*

199. *See* Olubunmi Faleye & Emery Trahan, Is What's Best for Employees Best for Shareholders? 1, 24 (2006), *available at* http:// ssrn.com/ abstract=888180 (noting that the market appears to value corporate concern for workers); Williams & Conley, *supra* note 195, at 78–79 (discussing trends that have altered society's expectations regarding business).

200. Timothy Smith, Institutional and Social Investors Find Common Ground, J. Investing, Fall 2005, at 57 (noting that social and environmental issues have been integrated into concerns of institutional investors, leading such investors to support proposals related to these issues); *see also* 2006 Proxy Season Report, *supra* note 63, at 41 (noting that the most recent proxy seasons were characterized by increased collaboration between proponents of social responsibility issues and other investors); Inst'l S'holder Servs., 2004 Postseason Report: A New Corporate Governance World: From Confrontation to Constructive Dialogue 28, *available at* http://www.issproxy.com/pdf/2004ISSPSR.pdf [hereinafter 2004 Proxy Season Report] (noting that increased support for social proposals stems from the greater support from corporate leaders who have come to view such proposals as meriting the same attention as other aspects of corporate governance).

201. *See* Smith, *supra* note 200, at 1 (noting increased collaboration between traditional shareholders and efforts by labor unions, religious investors, and socially responsible investment companies, which have blurred the lines between social and governance issues).

INDEX